Learning through STORYTELLING (in) Higher Education

Using Reflection & Experience to Improve Learning

JANICE McDRURY • MAXINE ALTERIO

KOGAN PAGE

London and Sterling, VA

First published in New Zealand in 2002 by The Dunmore Press Limited entitled *Learning through Storytelling: Using reflection and experience in higher education contexts*

First published in Great Britain and the United States in 2003 by Kogan Page Limited entitled *Learning Through Storytelling in Higher Education: Using reflection and experience to improve learning*

120 Pentonville Road
London N1 9JN
UK
www.kogan-page.co.uk

22883 Quicksilver Drive
Sterling VA 20166-2012
USA

© Dunmore Press Limited, 2002
© Janice McDrury and Maxine Alterio, 2002, 2003

ISBN 0 7494 4038 4

British Library Cataloguing in Publication Data

A CIP record for this book is available from the British Library.

Library of Congress Cataloging-in-Publication Data

McDrury, Janice, 1949-
  Learning through storytelling in higher education : using reflection
and experience to improve learning / Janice McDrury and Maxine Alterio.
    p. cm.
  ISBN 0-7494-4038-4
  1. Storytelling. 2. Education, Higher. 3. Experiential learning. I.
Alterio, Maxine, 1949- II. Title.
  LB1042.M33 2003
  378.1'2—dc21
                          2003005588

Printed and bound in Great Britain by Clays Ltd, St Ives plc

Contents

'Providing a rich and varied student experience is at the centre of higher education's goals. Janice and Maxine have authored an engaging, thought-provoking and practical text on the opportunities created through the use of storytelling as a reflective learning tool.'

Anne Pollock, Director of Quality Enhancement Services,
Napier University, Edinburgh

'Stories happen in the recounting of the events of our lives; we are the stories we tell. Drawing together elements from the muddle of experiences, and making sense of the interplay of facts and feelings, needs knowledge-able and skilful facilitation. Janice McDrury and Maxine Alterio have shown students and teachers how to develop rich partnerships in learning through the interweaving of storytelling and the active, dynamic process of reflection.'

Dr Elizabeth Farmer, Senior Lecturer, Department of
Nursing and Midwifery, University of Stirling

Foreword

It isn't very often that one comes across a book on academic pedagogy that engages one's attention to the extent that it is as difficult to put down as a novel. This book is a rare example of this phenomenon, bringing as it does a fresh and original perspective to the highly topical issue of making use of reflective practice in higher education to enhance the learning both of students and practitioners. The narrative instinct is a basic human one and it is impressive to see how the authors have used the process in structured and systematic ways to help learners to unpack what they have learned from their experiences in a variety of professional settings.

I have been aware of this book from its genesis, having had conversations with its authors in New Zealand while it was being drafted and celebrating with them when it was published by The Dunmore Press. I am therefore delighted to see that it is being brought to wider international attention through this publication by Kogan Page. I believe the authors have made a significant contribution to the ways in which we can understand the links between experience and learning that can impact positively on higher education internationally. This book shares many of the aims of the Institute for Learning and Teaching in Higher Education, which is a professional body for all who teach and support learning and was established to enhance the status of teaching, improve the experience of learning and support innovation in higher education. I am delighted therefore to commend this book to members and others who share our vision.

Sally Brown
Director of Membership Services
Institute for Learning and Teaching in Higher Education

Preface

Stories are everywhere. We hear them, we read them, we write them and we tell them. Perhaps on occasions we feel them. We use them to motivate others, to convey information and to share experience. We tell stories to entertain our friends and families, to connect with new people and to make sense of the world around us. As we tell stories we create opportunities to express views, reveal emotions and present aspects of our personal and professional lives. Frequently we engage in this uniquely human activity in creative ways and in doing so stimulate our imagination and enhance our memory and visualisation skills. Our ability to communicate not just our own experiences but the experiences of others enables us to transcend personal frameworks and take on wider perspectives. This attribute, together with its international, transhistorical and transcultural usage, makes storytelling a powerful learning tool. It is therefore not surprising that it has endured.

Authors from a range of backgrounds have suggested telling stories as a means of making sense of experience. These include psychologists (J. Bruner, 1986, 1987; E. Erickson, 1975; Polkinghorne, 1988), philosophers (MacIntyre, 1981; Ricoeur, 1984), historians (Clifford, 1986; Mink, 1978; White, 1973, 1981), anthropologists (E. Bruner, 1986; Rosaldo, 1989), psychoanalysts (Schafer, 1981; Spence, 1982), health professionals (Benner, 1984; Diekelmann, 1990, 1992; Sandelwoski, 1991; Taylor, 2000), therapists (Hart, 1995; Smith, 2001; White and Epston, 1990) and educators (Bishop and Glynn, 1999; Clandinin, 1993; Friend, 2000; Lauritzen and Jaeger, 1997; Mattingly, 1991; McCormack and Pamphilon, 1998; McEwan and Egan, 1995; Pendlebury, 1995; Reason and Hawkins, 1988; Van Manen, 1991).

Such widespread appeal has helped ease storytelling's transition into educational contexts. The emergence of a reflective paradigm in higher education sectors over the last two decades has also advanced storytelling's acceptance as a learning tool. Across and within disciplines, educators are using storytelling to stimulate students' critical thinking skills, encourage self-review and convey practice realities. In this book we link the art of storytelling with reflective processes and demonstrate how students can use this tool to inform, develop and advance their learning.

The book is divided into eleven chapters. In the initial chapters we explore the links between reflection, learning and storytelling in higher education and provide an account of how the ideas presented in the book were developed. In Chapter 4 we identify significant storytelling characteristics and explain how the choices they offer provide tellers with eight pathway options that are capable of achieving different learning outcomes. These aspects are then incoporated into our Reflective Learning through Storytelling Model. In the following five chapters we outline how our five-stage storytelling approach – *story finding*, *story telling*, *story expanding*, *story processing* and *story reconstructing* – can be used to facilitate student learning for the purpose of developing professional practice. We consider assessment and ethical issues in Chapter 10 and conclude, in Chapter 11, with a reflective account regarding our experience of writing a book about telling stories.

OUR AUDIENCE

We hope this book will have appeal for and be relevant to students and professionals working in a range of areas. We believe it has application for undergraduates preparing for professional practice and experienced practitioners seeking to advance their practice. We also envisage that health professionals supervising students in clinical practice settings, trainers working with clients and managers wanting to encourage a reflective culture, will find it a useful resource. Mentors, lecturers and staff and educational developers wanting to inculcate reflective practice approaches may also find its practical suggestions and theoretical components go some way towards addressing the gap between knowing storytelling can be used to learn about practice and actually using it in thoughtful and effective ways.

Acknowledgements

We offer our thanks to those family members and friends who gave their help and support in bringing this book into being. In particular, we would like to acknowledge the assistance of Professor Keith Ballard who gave us thoughtful feedback on theoretical components and Associate Professor Terry Crooks who provided us with useful comments on assessment and ethical aspects. Our thanks also go to Kate Doherty and Martha Morseth for their assistance with our early drafts.

For the first storytellers we encountered: our parents, Mavis and Arthur McDrury, and Lorna and John Ferns.

1 Introduction

There are possibly as many ways of beginning books as there are of starting stories. While storytelling can occur spontaneously, the techniques some writers use to draw readers into text parallel the ways many storytellers engage listeners in the oral process. Words are chosen and arranged on the page or presented verbally in an attempt to capture the attention of a particular group of readers or listeners. How effectively writers and storytellers manage this endeavour is dependent on many factors, one being the ability to translate knowledge, experience and intuition into words and images that appeal to the intended audience. Ideally each significant word, or cluster of words, serves two purposes: first, it contributes to the meaning of what is being conveyed, and second, it moves the text or story forward in ways that engage the audience. Providing adequate contextual information is another useful technique because it helps readers or listeners connect with aspects that are meaningful to them.

The context for this book is higher education and our primary intention is to suggest ways in which storytelling can be used effectively as a learning tool. For this purpose we draw on our experiences as researchers, lecturers and students, and as individuals who have been interested in, and surrounded by, stories from an early age. Throughout our adult years we have enjoyed numerous conversations with friends and colleagues about how storytelling impacts on our personal and professional lives. In recent years we have worked with stories in formalised ways to enhance student learning. During this period we have talked with and gathered feedback from students and colleagues who have used our storytelling processes. These interactions and subsequent feedback helped shape our thinking as we prepared to embark on the writing of this book. *Learning Through Storytelling* is the result of many such interactions, including the happy coincidence of our own professional journeys coming together in the same place, at the right time.

OUR RATIONALE

Our intention is to link the art of storytelling with reflective learning processes and to demonstrate how educators might use the ideas, strategies and processes we present to prepare students better for the rigours and uncertainties inherent in professional practice. We are convinced that storytelling has enabled us to learn from experience throughout our lives and we have discovered that it can also be used in meaningful, enjoyable and creative ways to facilitate learning in higher education settings.

The more we used storytelling with students the more we realised its application to lifelong learning. Around the same time we also began to pay attention to informal stories. We noticed what stories were told where, what responses were given in particular settings and how the way stories were told influenced the outcomes they achieved. Our enthusiasm to learn more about the nature of storytelling and, in particular, how to use it formally in higher education contexts led us on a journey of inquiry. We examined storytelling characteristics in more detail, developed a storytelling pathway model, and designed, then used, three formalised processes with research participants, undergraduate and postgraduate students and interested colleagues. We presented our findings at conferences, published papers and ran workshops on storytelling. This led to the development and implementation of the five-stage learning-through-storytelling approach we describe in this text. As we formulated our concepts, strategies and processes, we learned about storytelling along with our students and colleagues and we are eternally grateful for their enthusiastic participation.

Our thinking about storytelling took another significant leap when we embarked on this book. We therefore welcome the opportunity to place our ideas about storytelling in a public arena for others to adapt and develop further. Still passionate about the way we relate to, work with and learn from stories, we offer this book as a resource to anyone interested in using storytelling as a learning tool.

OUR STORIES

During the writing of this book we became increasingly aware of the many influences that had contributed to our interest in storytelling. Our families and the way they told or did not tell stories, how we had viewed reading and writing-related activities during childhood, our school experiences, why we chose particular careers and most importantly what place stories had and still have in our lives. In keeping with our theme we now share these influences in story form.

Janice

Sharing of experience through stories was an important part of my early life. The wonder and joy of hearing adventures set in other places and times alerted me to different worlds, different realities. My parents shared snippets of the joys and sorrows that impacted on their childhood in the country. The simple pleasures and ability to create times of relaxation contrasted with the harsh reality of the depression years, limited resources and ailing parents. While most of these stories were contained within the realm of day-to-day activities, there were also the significant events over time where themes and characters were more constant. Dad's experience of being employed by the Ministry of Works to put power lines across the Southern Alps and Mum's experience during the war years became epic adventures.

However, there were also stories that were not told that had a significant impact on my life. In particular, Dad's war stories. His life was, in many ways, shaped by the years in places such as Egypt, Rome and Palestine. Yet he talked little of death and destruction, or of the illnesses he contracted that remained with him throughout life, and only occasionally did he recount humorous events that gave me brief insight into the harshness of his reality.

For me, stories occurred primarily in the oral tradition, through listening and telling. Stories were shared by people who had experienced them first or second-hand and were willing to share the events, the feelings and the outcomes. Most important to me was being able to talk with tellers, to seek clarification, elaboration or expansion. In this way I had opportunities to somehow become part of these stories and gain understanding and insight.

Written stories had little appeal. I struggled to learn to read and had limited interest in the banal school texts I was capable of reading. However, I was happy to have stories read to me as I could then talk about them, wonder what else could have happened or discuss alternative approaches. Stories were a beginning point for dialogue. Predictably the demand during school years for me to write stories held little relevance. I had no academic concept of developing a theme, uncovering a plot, creating suspension or discovering resolution. Most of my school essays were jointly written with my mother, with her attempting to create and extract a story, and me being happy just to write down whatever words were necessary! It wasn't until doing a stage two education paper at Massey University as a mature student that I discovered there were different learning styles. This insight unlocked my ability to write.

So, with little interest in written stories but a strong oral tradition, I entered nursing. I found an immediate match with many other students. Nursing has a strong oral tradition and storytelling became our key debriefing tool. The hours spent sharing the joys, sorrows, embarrassing moments and funny situations enabled us to make sense of our world and also discover how colleagues were dealing with their realities. The nurses' home provided a wonderful storytelling space. There were always tellers and listeners – all hours of the day and night.

Storytelling remained with me over my years of nursing and was carried into the teaching/learning environment in a very natural and spontaneous way. I used stories as a means of sharing experience, enabling others to view the nursing reality, and demonstrating ways of being with patients and their families in their moments of sadness and joy.

Once I embarked on my PhD journey, storytelling began to take on new meaning. I was interested in learning from experience, especially reflective experience. I was challenged to develop tools to enhance reflection, and storytelling seemed obvious as it was the means nurses used spontaneously. I listened to stories that were shared over coffee and lunch breaks. I dialogued on stories from practice with students and colleagues. Gradually I began to wonder about when, where, how and why stories were told. I was also interested in the type of stories told and what outcomes they could achieve. My thinking on storytelling is informed by these experiences and forms the basis of what I share in this book.

Maxine

I have always derived pleasure from, and been challenged by, the power of reflection and, in particular, the forms of reflection associated with reading fiction, engaging in creative writing activities and sharing stories. Encouraged as a child to value 'daydreaming' as a worthwhile form of thinking, I created fantasy worlds that stimulated and stretched my imagination. These worlds were often played out in daring and entertaining ways. Attempting to fly from a henhouse roof, walking a tightrope strung between a shed and garage, and riding a one-wheel bicycle as part of a circus act started as imagined possibilities and ended as thoughtfully choreographed physical adventures.

Active participation in my father's creative interpretations of well-known stories was also very much part of my childhood. He acted out stories such as 'The Three Billy Goats Gruff' by becoming the troll and hiding under the kitchen table while encouraging me to run across it saying 'No, no, don't eat me, wait for my little sisters, they're much juicier'. Original stories were also part of my parents' repertoire. Imaginary characters such as *Hairy Fairy* accompanied me through childhood and helped nourish my interest in storytelling.

Once I was able to read I devoured books, transporting my mind to countries I had not known existed and to lifestyles that intrigued and mystified me. I became interested in why characters behaved in certain ways, frequently asking myself how I would have acted if placed in the same situation. Immersed in the lives of fictional characters, I shared their adventures and became familiar with the landscapes in which their stories unfolded. At this stage I was convinced that books could provide everything I wanted to know.

Writing my own stories was a natural progression. I wrote scripts for plays, circuses and puppet shows, a consuming and enjoyable activity that helped me survive many long Southland winters. These stories were rarely edited. My focus was on content, not style, grammatical details or spelling.

Attending school seemed like an intrusion because it interrupted my writing and reading life. I considered school regimented, boring and rule-bound. For a while I believed that teachers were harming my brain by requiring me to do mathematics, reading or spelling at certain times. Forty-minute periods for these subjects did not sit well with my natural 'learn what you want when you want' approach. I felt compelled to suppress my creative spirit. By the time I reached secondary level I viewed school-based learning as something that had to be endured for legal reasons.

I was in my late twenties, and the mother of three small children, before I considered formal education might have something to offer. With the encouragement of my brother I enrolled in a University Entrance English class at the local polytechnic, where I would later teach for seven years. I loved this class. What made the difference? The time was right for me and I had a teacher who was student-centred. The following year I did Bursary English through the Correspondence School and a year later enrolled in Stage One Education at Massey University.

I was an ideal extramural student, being motivated, able to set my own goals and happy to learn when and how I wanted. I took papers in education, psychology, linguistics and English, eventually completing my undergraduate degree as a part-time student at the University of Otago. A Diploma of Teaching (Tertiary) and a Master of Arts (by thesis only) followed. To fulfil my thesis requirements I explored how practitioners from four professions used journalling and storytelling as tools of reflection, analysis, self-evaluation and as ways of initiating and supporting change to professional practice. Once again my three childhood loves, writing and reading and storytelling, were integral to my life although I did not fully appreciate how this came about until I was thoroughly immersed in my research project.

Prior to and during my research, I was also reading and thinking about reflection. The concept made complete sense to me and provided me with a framework for my teaching practice. By this stage I was employed as a staff development coordinator, having held various roles in the higher education sector.

My interest in exploring storytelling as a professional development tool continued to grow. I began presenting my ideas at conferences and facilitating workshops locally, nationally and internationally. In my personal life, I continued to read widely and write short stories, poems and fragments of novels. Several short stories have been broadcast on radio. Others have been published in literary journals in New Zealand and the United Kingdom. A few have won or been shortlisted for prizes.

Finally, my professional life and my personal interests have intersected. Reading, writing, listening to, telling and working with stories is, for me, integral to the learning process. It is from this perspective that I offer some ideas, activities and processes for educators to consider when encouraging students to learn through storytelling.

BOOK OUTLINE

So far in this chapter we have introduced the idea of learning through storytelling, given our rationale for writing the book and described how our interest in the topic came from a range of influences and experiences. In the following two chapters we review the literature which has informed our storytelling approach. In Chapter 2 we focus on reflection and learning while in Chapter 3 we provide an overview of the storytelling literature. In Chapter 4 we position our storytelling approach within a constructivist paradigm, introduce a Reflective Learning through Storytelling Model, present the concept of formalised storytelling through our Pathways Model (McDrury and Alterio, 2001) and describe the interrelationships between storytelling processes and cathartic/reflective learning outcomes.

To demonstrate how students can use stories to bring about constructive learning, we offer a five-stage approach, beginning in Chapter 5 where we suggest how a storytelling culture can be created by introducing students to a range of activities to assist in *story finding*, the first stage in our model. In Chapter 6, the *story telling* stage, we outline one way to move students from listening to stories, to telling them, to writing exemplars based on practice experiences. Chapter 7 describes how to introduce students to several theories of reflection for the purpose of managing the third stage of our model, *story expanding*. In this chapter we also provide an exercise to assist students with meta-analysis of stories and reflection. We develop our ideas about formalised storytelling and introduce the stage of *story processing* in Chapter 8 with accounts of how focused reflective dialogue, on and around practice stories, can lead to significant learning. We describe how students can share their stories using a formalised storytelling process. Stories emerging from spontaneous drawing activities are also explored as are reflective processes used to bring about change. In Chapter 9 our focus is on *story reconstructing*, the fifth stage in our Reflective Learning through Storytelling Model. At this stage a group storytelling process, used to gain multiple perspectives on practice events, is outlined.

The purpose of Chapters 5 to 9 is to provide students with a storytelling approach that gradually moves them through levels of reflective learning. We also provide educators with templates to assist in this process. Our intention is to demonstrate how storytelling can be used as a learning tool at different levels, in different ways, for different purposes.

In Chapter 10, we consider assessment and ethical issues. In this challenging chapter, we outline our views on assessing storytelling and provide practical suggestions on how assessment might be managed. Ethical issues ranging from who owns stories once they are shared, to how students can be supported within formalised storytelling situations, are also explored. We draw our journey of inquiry to a close in Chapter 11 by reflecting on the process of writing a book about telling stories. We describe how our views on storytelling shifted as we challenged our own practices through discussion on drafts, feedback from colleagues and students, and inevitably, by engaging in self-review. Writing this book did not take place in isolation. It has been a social process and therefore, in the spirit of collaborative endeavour, we invite you, as reader, to reflect on your storytelling experiences as you engage with this text.

2 Storytelling Influences

Our work with stories has been influenced by current views on the nature of learning (Brockbank and McGill, 1998; Brookfield and Preskill, 1999; Entwistle, 1988, 1996; Fry, Ketteridge and Marshall, 1999; McGee and Fraser, 2001; Moon, 1999; Race, 2000; Ramsden, 1992). Views about learning have shifted in recent years to accommodate the reflective movement. Given this shift, and while recognising that the concept of reflection has been widely published (Atkins and Murphy, 1993; Boud, Keogh and Walker, 1985; Boyd and Fales, 1983; Cowan, 1998; Holly, 1984; Moon 1999; Schön, 1983,1987), we begin by summarising how it has influenced our views on student learning.

REFLECTION

The role reflection plays in education is currently attracting considerable attention and debate throughout the world. Educators from a range of disciplines are embracing a reflective outlook and encouraging students to learn about themselves and their areas of study by engaging in reflective activities. While acknowledging that many educators working at all levels promote reflection, our focus is on how it can be facilitated in higher education contexts. In this setting students enrolled in undergraduate and postgraduate programmes are often required to undertake clinical placements or equivalent work experience. These learning opportunities, together with the life experiences students bring to formal learning environments, provide educators with rich and relevant opportunities to make meaningful links between theory and practice.

The traditional model of educating aspiring professionals solely within the confines of an educational institution, and separating 'knowing what' (theory) from 'knowing how' (practice), has been challenged extensively (Boud, Keogh and Walker 1985; Bruner, 1985; Eraut, 1994; Habermas, 1987; Heron, 1989; Schön, 1983). The traditional model endured because it was believed that 'practical knowledge was context bound while theoretical knowledge was comparatively context free' (Eraut, 1994: 50). We now recognise that theoretical knowledge *is* affected by context and 'a significant proportion of the learning associated with any change in practice takes place in its context of use' (Eraut, 1994: 37).

Eraut (1994) also questions the belief that we acquire knowledge for later use. He suggests that 'not only does an idea get reinterpreted during use, but it may even need to be used before it can acquire any significant meaning for the user' (p.51). Such a perspective suggests any meaning is likely to be influenced by previous contexts and will require further intellectual effort before it can be transferred into another setting. This view highlights some of the complexities associated with the nature of professional knowledge. There is increased acceptance that 'important aspects of professional competence and expertise cannot be satisfactorily represented in propositional form and embedded in a publicly accessible knowledge base' (Eraut, 1994: 15). Current thinking suggests a much broader framework is needed.

The notion of reflective practice providing such a framework has appeal because of its potential for personalised application. It offers one way to access what practitioners know and do intuitively but cannot easily share, referred to by Polanyi (1967) as 'tacit knowledge'. Argyris and Schön (1974) found it helped to reveal discrepancies between 'espoused theories', what practitioners think is happening and why, and 'theories in use', what is actually occurring in practice.

Attempts to capture tacit knowledge and to find ways of reducing the gap between espoused theories and theories in use contributed to the development of a reflective paradigm. Schön (1983), in particular, highlighted the significance and value of reflection in raising awareness of tacit knowledge and transforming knowing-in-action to knowledge-in-action. Reflecting on practice is recognised as one method which can be used to locate differences between espoused theories and theories in use and initiate and support new learning (Schön, 1983).

Numerous theorists and practitioners have advocated the use of reflection as a learning tool and have analysed the processes of reflection (Boud, Keogh and Walker 1985; Butler, 1994; Coutts-Jarman, 1993; Holly, 1984; Mezirow, 1981; Schön, 1983, 1987, 1991; Van Manen, 1977) but definitions of the concept are relatively sparse. Boyd and Fales (1983) maintain that 'reflective learning is the process of internally examining and exploring an issue of concern, triggered by an experience, which creates and clarifies meaning in terms of self, and which results in a changed conceptual perspective' (p.99). Boud, Keogh and Walker (1985) say 'reflection, in the context of learning, is a generic term for those intellectual and affective activities in which individuals engage to explore their experiences in order to lead to new understandings and appreciations' (p.19). While Kemmis maintains reflection can have an emancipatory effect by encouraging inquirers to engage in proactive initiatives within their learning contexts, he differentiates between reflection and passive contemplation. Kemmis (1985) claims reflection 'is a social process, serves human interests, is a political process' and is a 'practice which expresses our power to reconstitute social life by the way we participate in communication, decision-making and social action' (p.140). Moon (1999), after undertaking a comprehensive overview of the literature, concludes that 'reflection seems to be a form of mental processing with a purpose and/or an anticipated outcome that is applied to relatively complicated or unstructured ideas for which there is not an obvious solution' (p.98).

These definitions have some commonalities in that the process of reflection involves the self and the consequence of reflection is a changed conceptual viewpoint. Moon (1999) contends, however, that while the activity of reflecting appears to be understood, problems are encountered when attempts are made to define the concept in formal or academic terms. She maintains that: 'The existence of different accounts of reflection without a common definition at their root means that particular features associated with the term have been accentuated or diminished in the definition of the word in order to apply it to the topic in hand' (p.92).

Moon attributes this situation to the haphazard proliferation of thought (knowledge and speculation) which surrounds reflection. While stressing that there is nothing wrong with such development, she suggests it does create difficulties for those who want to investigate the concept from a theoretical perspective or apply it to a new domain of activity. Various authors also have different perspectives on aspects of the reflective process.

Reason and Hawkins (1988) see explanation and expression as two ways to reflect on and process experience. They describe explanation (similar to empirical/analytical) as the mode of classifying, conceptualising and building theories from experience, and expression (similar to hermeneutic/phenomenological) as the mode of enabling meaning of experience to become apparent. When students operate in explanation mode, their stance becomes one of detachment. Concepts are discovered or created and applied to theoretical models. Expression mode, however, requires students to be actively involved in their experiences so they can create and communicate meaning. When students are encouraged to learn in this way, they often encounter aspects of self-study.

Dilthey's (1977) notion of reflecting on one's life as an ongoing autobiographical activity that acts as a sediment for actions and decisions is used by Witherell (1991) to demonstrate how reflection influences learning processes. She draws our attention to the way personal meanings constantly shift because they are contingent on context, and oneself and others, a view that links with Vygotsky's (1987) 'zone of proximal development'.

These views connect with Kemmis (1985), who links types of reflective activity to three forms of thinking: technical, practical and critical. He maintains that technical reasoning focuses on application of specific skills in a stable environment, practical reasoning encompasses a holistic approach, and critical thinking, the most complex level, takes a dialectic approach by addressing the social and historical contexts in relation to an event.

According to Kemmis (1985), reflection is dialectical in several ways: first, by striving to understand how the actions of individuals (informed by critical reflection) shape history and how the type and content of thought is shaped by history; second, by considering how individuals' thought processes are shaped by a social and cultural context; and finally, how the social and cultural context is itself shaped by the thoughts and actions of individuals. Reflection, as Kemmis (1985) posits, can be described as 'meta-thinking' (thinking about thinking) for it has the potential to propel us into further thought followed on occasion by action. Mezirow (1981), however, reminds us that while reflection alone does not ensure change, it can contribute to the possibility of change.

One difficulty with the reflective process itself is evident in the differing accounts of reflective levels presented by authors. Mezirow (1981) proposes seven levels of reflection arranged in a hierarchy, from reflectivity (which is an awareness of thoughts and feelings) through to theoretical reflexivity (which involves challenging one's underlying assumptions, resulting in a changed perspective). Schön (1991) suggests three levels: conscious reflection, criticism and action. Hatton and Smith (1995) have drawn on Schön's (1983, 1987, 1991) work to develop a five-level approach. They have identified technical, descriptive, dialogical and critical reflection which they contend represent increasingly more sophisticated levels of what Schön

(1983) refers to as reflection-on-action which occurs after the event. Their final level, which they also attribute to Schön (1983, 1987), is reflection-in-action which takes place in the work setting during the incident. Other authors maintain that intuition, defined as understanding without rationale, also plays a central function (Atkinson and Claxton, 2000; Benner and Tanner, 1987; Goodman, 1984).

Differences in how reflection is perceived are predominantly in terminology, detail, and the extent to which the process is arranged in a hierarchy. In a review article about reflection, Atkins and Murphy (1993) identify three key stages, which are shared by most authors. The first stage is characterised by inner discomfort, according to Boud, Keogh and Walker (1985), and the experience of surprise, according to Schön, (1991). The associated thoughts and feelings arise when there is a discrepancy between what is known and what is happening in a particular situation.

The second stage involves processes of critical analysis of feelings and knowledge that Mezirow (1981) refers to as conceptual, psychic and theoretical reflexivity and Boud, Keogh and Walker (1985) as association, integration, validation and appropriation. Analysis at this stage may include the examination or generation of new knowledge. The final stage includes the emergence of a new perspective of the situation. Mezirow (1981) refers to this stage as perspective transformation, a term he uses to describe how we can become critically aware that our assumptions about the environment in which we live constrain the way we see our relationships and ourselves. He suggests we can come to a transformed perspective by either gaining sudden insight or by a series of ongoing shifts in assumptions, which enable us to form new perspectives.

These three stages are integrated and the outcome of such reflection is learning. We must be aware, however, that reflection is not simply an individual process. Like language, it is a social process. Haigh (2000) supports Brookfield's view that reflective processes become more productive when others are involved, and maintains that questioning is central to productive reflection:

> When such questioning is facilitative, it prompts practitioners to go beyond their first thoughts and taken for granted ideas about situations, experiences and their own actions (or inactions), to critically examine underpinning beliefs, assumptions and values, and to generate and evaluate their own solutions to their own problems (p.92).

Haigh (2000) suggests there are three prerequisites essential to effective reflection: 'belief in the value of reflection, knowledge of what would be a worthwhile focus for reflection and a rich repertoire of reflection skills' (p.95). As an interactive, social process, reflection cannot be understood without reference to action or context.

Schön (1991) argues that professionals encounter complex and diverse situations in everyday practice; therefore, straightforward rational approaches to learning are not sufficient. Reflective practice, according to Schön (1983), stresses the importance of experience and plays down the theoretical component. Knowing and doing are synonymous to Schön (1983). He explains:

> When we go about the spontaneous, intuitive performance of the actions of everyday life, we show ourselves to be knowledgeable in a special way. Often we cannot say what it is that we know. When we try to describe it we find ourselves at a loss, or we produce descriptions that are obviously inappropriate. Our knowledge is ordinarily tacit, implicit in our patterns of action and in our feel for the stuff with which we are dealing. It seems right to say that our knowing is *in* our action (p.49).

Schön (1983) contends that practitioners often draw on practical experience in a highly intuitive way. Reflection according to Schön (1983) is triggered when a situation is somehow different and therefore warrants further thought. In Benner's (1984) work with nurses she found a similar trigger produced an intuitive feeling of unease that something was not right. Like Schön (1983), we acknowledge that reflection or thoughtful deliberation influences our actions. What we are less certain of is the role reflection has in the process of learning, a relationship Moon (1999) also identifies as yet to be satisfactorily explained.

Moon (1999) maintains that 'the existence of this gap between an identification of the nature of reflection and the processes of learning means that many applications of reflection in education and professional situations are guided by assumptions or guesswork' (Preface: ix). She attempts to address this gap by drawing reflection from the realms of intuition and instinct and relating it more closely with the process of learning. Moon (1999) offers an input process–outcome model of reflection. Put simply this model has inputs described as 'what we know' which she suggests are 'processed by means of reflection to create a series of outcomes that then represent the purposes for which we reflect' (p.99).

Moon (1999) also alludes to the capacity to 'be reflective' which she believes is 'an orientation to the activities of life rather than a mental process itself' (p.100). She suggests that educators wanting to discover how reflection can be better used to improve student learning should begin by understanding the learning process itself.

LEARNING

Many theories of learning have informed our thinking and the ways in which we use storytelling with students. In particular, we have benefited greatly from the works of Kolb (1984); Boud, Keogh and Walker (1985); Boud, Cohen and Walker (1993); Schön (1983, 1987); Moon, (1999); Entwistle (1988, 1996); and Vygotsky (1987). We now provide brief accounts of these contributions as they pertain to our focus.

Kolb's (1984) experiential learning cycle brings reflection into prominence by naming a stage based on the concept. This four-stage cycle involves four adaptive learning modes – concrete experience, reflective observation, abstract conceptualisation and active experimentation. It has been used extensively in learning communities and is based on the premise that an experience such as attending a course, observing a demonstration or receiving assistance from a peer or teacher does not in itself guarantee that learning will occur. For meaningful learning to take place the student must reflect on experience, generalise the experience to other situations, decide how to translate learning into action, then evaluate the outcome of that action.

While Kolb (1984) acknowledges that students may vary in their abilities to perform in different stages of the cycle and attributes these differences to preferred learning styles, he stresses the importance of completing each stage. Although he does not expand on the concept of reflection, he does indicate that its quality has a significant impact on the degree to which students will progress in their learning.

In our experience, students new to the experiential learning cycle often find the reflective observation stage the most challenging. There may be many reasons, some of them embedded in the students themselves, others linked to teaching and learning environments, and still others connected to the nature of reflection.

We have already acknowledged the contribution Boud, Keogh and Walker (1985) made to our understanding of reflection. Our thinking about experience and its relationship to learning was also informed by Boud, Cohen and Walker (1993). As we developed our ideas about using storytelling as a learning tool we were mindful of five propositions that underpin their views on experience and learning.

1.   Experience is the foundation of, and stimulus for, learning.
2.   Learners actively construct their experience.
3.   Learning is a holistic process.
4.   Learning is socially and culturally constructed.
5.   Learning is influenced by the socio-emotional context in which it occurs.

(p.8–14)

Boud, Cohen and Walker's (1993) emphasis on socio-emotional aspects addressed a concern we had about the omission of feelings and emotions in higher education contexts where teaching and learning strategies tend to focus on intellectual and practical pursuits. We concur with the view 'that denial of feelings is denial of learning' (Boud, Keogh and Walker 1985: 15). In our experience the most significant learning frequently takes place during or after powerfully emotional events. This phenomena is recognised by Postle (1983) and Criticos (1983) who suggest that had we known beforehand what emotional chaos we might encounter in some situations, we may well have avoided these learning opportunities. Yet these very traumatic experiences often yield the most significant learning.

Indeed Schön (1983, 1987) asserts that one of the hallmarks of a reflective practitioner is to seek out connections between thoughts and feelings, an aspect we wanted to incorporate into our storytelling processes. We have also benefited from Schön's (1983, 1987) work in other ways. His ideas about the construction of professional knowledge, in particular his thoughts on how professionals use intuitive capacities to reconceptualise situations or reframe problems, together with the emphasis he places on professional creativity, initially encouraged us to use reflective strategies such as collaborative journalling and spontaneous drawing with students. Our experiences and subsequent learning from using these reflective activities contributed to our interest in developing reflective storytelling processes.

Searching for ways to make meaningful links between learning and reflection also interests Moon (1999). Informed by the general literature on learning, including deep and surface approaches (Entwistle, 1996), the theory of human interests (Habermas, 1971) and perspective transformation (Mezirow, 1981), Moon (1999) identified a five-stage map of learning: noticing, making sense, making meaning, working with meaning and transformative meaning. Moon (1999) acknowledges that her map is speculative, although 'based on theory, empirical work and observation, the work on deep and surface learning, and the relationship between the two and the outcomes of that learning' (p.136), but puts it forward to promote thinking about the processes of learning and reflection on learning.

Entwistle's (1996) revised descriptions of surface, strategic and deep approaches to learning influenced the development of Moon's (1999) map. Surface learning, which has coping with course requirements as its intention, clearly states the absence of reflection ('studying *without reflecting* on either purpose or strategy'), cited by Moon (1999), as a key attribute. Entwistle (1996) believes the strategic approach is more controversial given that it is only evident when learning is being assessed. Ramsden (1992) offers a counter view, suggesting that strategic learners utilise deep and surface approaches, depending on their reading of what is required, to achieve high marks in assessed work. This belief fits with Biggs's (1999) claim that students adopt learning strategies to suit their particular settings.

The deep approach, which is our focus given its role in reflective learning, is a strategy requiring high-order cognitive skills and the ability to think conceptually. It is driven by the intention to understand ideas by relating them to previous knowledge and experience, looking for patterns and underlying principles, checking evidence and relating it to conclusions, examining logic and argument cautiously and critically, and becoming actively interested in course content (Entwistle, 1996). Phrases used to describe the deep approach ('looking for patterns', 'examining cautiously and critically'), cited by Moon (1999), are indicative of reflective activity; hence, its usefulness for our purpose.

As these authors note, learning does not occur in isolation. Students' realities are, as Bishop (2000) asserts, central to the learning process. Therefore, in multi-ethnic societies such as Aotearoa New Zealand, learning strategies are required which recognise, value and sustain the cultures, values and knowledge of all students (Adams, Clark, Codd, O'Neill, Openshaw and Waitere-Ang, 2000). This view is supported by Kalantzis and Cape (1999), who contend that in order to maintain and value diverse student backgrounds, 'learning processes need to recruit, rather than attempt to ignore and erase, the different subjectivities students bring to learning' (p.27).

Vygotsky (1987), the Russian psychologist turned educator who emphasised the social context of thinking, shares the view that the contexts in which individuals operate or with which they connect significantly impact on their learning potential. Jerome Bruner (1987), another highly influential educator, has commented that, in his view, Vygotsky's (1987) concept of human development is also a theory of education, and his theory of education is also a theory of cultural transmission commonly known as socio-cultural theory. Bruner (1987) bases this belief on the notion that education for Vygotsky means development of both self and humankind. Many educators view Vygotsky's primary contribution as developing a general approach that brought education, as a fundamentally human activity, wholly into a theory of psychological development (Moll, 1990). This development resulted in educators considering how educational practices might constrain or advance thinking and contributed to the call for new, innovative and advanced learning approaches (Moll, 1990).

Central to Vygotsky's (1987) socio-cultural theory is the importance of context in relation to learning. Context, also known as 'activity setting', provides the medium in which students discover meaning through social encounter. These encounters enable students to become familiar with the nuances of their contexts and gain assistance with problems beyond their competence. This construct, the zone of proximal development (ZPD), influenced the way educators saw themselves, their students and the artificial learning and teaching environments in which they interacted. Vygotsky (1987) describes the ZPD as 'the distance between the actual developmental level as determined by independent problem solving and the level of potential development as determined through problem-solving under adult guidance or in collaboration with more capable peers' (p.86).

There are four distinct stages.

1. Performance is assisted by more capable others.
2. Performance is assisted by self.
3. Performance is developed, automatised and fossilised.
4. De-automatisation of performance leads to recursion through the zone of proximal development.

(Gallimore and Tharp, 1988: 184–186)

For a detailed description of this model we refer you to Tharp and Gallimore (1988). For our purposes we note that through his self–social model, Vygotsky (1987) alerts us to the fact that educational environments are social creations and can therefore be altered. He also reminds us how easily human capabilities can be underestimated when analysed in isolation and points out that the social and cultural resources we carry as human beings are potential learning tools. These tools, such as spoken and written language, he believes determine humans' relations with their environment and with themselves and are produced through social activity (Hedegaard, 1990), a view we subscribe to and which has influenced our development as educators.

Our purpose in this chapter has been to explore the links between reflection and learning. In subsequent chapters, we demonstrate how these authors and aspects of their work informed our thinking and, in doing so, shaped the way we developed our storytelling approach. We now review the literature on storytelling.

3 Storytelling Developments

Although the reflective strategies educators use to facilitate student learning vary according to personal preference, purpose and context, the literature suggests storytelling is gaining popularity in higher education (Clandinin and Connolly, 1998; Grant and Friend, 1996; McEwan and Egan, 1995; Pendlebury, 1995; and Witherell and Noddings, 1991). In this chapter we review the literature to establish what constitutes storytelling and report on narrative developments as they pertain to learning in higher education contexts.

WHAT IS STORYTELLING?

Storytelling is a uniquely human experience that enables us to convey, through the language of words, aspects of ourselves and others, and the worlds, real or imagined, that we inhabit. Stories enable us to come to know these worlds and our place in them given that we are all, to some degree, constituted by stories: stories about ourselves, our families, friends and colleagues, our communities, our cultures, our place in history. Hardy's (1977: 13) observation that 'we dream in narrative, daydream in narrative, remember, anticipate, hope, despair, believe, doubt, plan, revise, criticise, construct, gossip, learn, hate and live by narrative', reveals how pervasive and integral stories are to our lives. As Lodge (1990: 4) comments, 'narrative is one of the fundamental sense-making operations of the mind, and would appear to be both peculiar to and universal among human beings'. Byatt (2000: 166) concurs, saying storytelling is 'as much part of human nature as breath and the circulation of blood', a view echoed by

Barthes (1977: 79) who says 'it is simply there, like life itself'. Given its power, and the way it touches individual lives, it is worth noting McEwan and Egan's (1995: viii) observation: 'A narrative, and that particular form of narrative that we call a story, deals not just in facts or ideas or theories, or even dreams, fears and hopes, but in facts, theories, and dreams from the perspective of someone's life and in the context of someone's emotions'.

This emotional aspect is one of storytelling's strengths, and perhaps one reason for its recent resurgence, given the call for educators to acknowledge, value and draw on the emotional realities of students' lives (Boud, Keogh and Walker, 1985; Beatty, 2000), an area we explore later in this chapter.

The fundamental human need to recount and explore experience, including affective components, frequently results in the composition of some form of narrative, often a story that describes actions, emotions and outcomes in temporal sequence. Such stories place events in narrative contexts and by doing so assign them particular meanings (Tappan and Brown, 1991). As White (1991: 1) suggests: 'narrative might well be considered a solution to a problem of general human concern, namely the problem of how to translate *knowing* into *telling*, the problem of fashioning human experience into a form assimilable to structures of meaning that are generally human'.

Indeed, Van Manen (1991: 204) thinks of storytelling as 'a form of everyday theorising'. Others agree that we can create and present theoretical accounts through storytelling (Bishop and Glynn, 1999; Clandinin, 1985; Lauritzen and Jaeger, 1997; McEwan and Egan, 1995; Pagano, 1991; White, 1991). Noddings and Witherell (1991: 279) explain: 'stories can help us understand by making the abstract concrete and accessible'.

Stockhausen (1992: 9) believes storytelling's aim is to 'capture, code, and validate the (generative) knowledge born of experience, observation and intuition'. The role of experience in the formation of knowledge is recognised by Heron (1981) who maintains that all modes of inquiry begin with experiential knowing, an observation Kolb (1984) acted on when he constructed his experiential learning cycle described in Chapter 2 and widely used by educators.

According to Reason and Hawkins (1988), storytelling can be viewed as a mode of inquiry because it involves cooperative activity, has a qualitative focus and encompasses holistic perspectives. They also maintain it can be used 'either to explain or to express; to analyse or to understand' (p.79), a view they arrived at after sharing stories with colleagues and processing them in different ways. Reason and his colleagues discovered the more they worked with their personal stories, the more learning power their stories had, leading them to conclude, 'existentially we create our own meanings from events' (p.98).

Making meaning through stories is for Didion (1979), a writer and essayist, intricately linked to living. 'We tell ourselves stories in order to live. We live . . . by the imposition of a narrative line upon disparate images, by the "ideas" with which we have learned to freeze the shifting phantas-magoria which is our actual experience' (p.11).

Our lives, as Winter, Buck and Sobiechowska (1999: 21) contend, are 'steeped in stories' and always have been. As Parkin (1998: 1) notes, 'stories, metaphors, myths and legends, together with their relatives – anecdotes, similes and analogies – have all been used as methods for communication and teaching since time began'. Before the written word, storytellers passed the cumulative wisdom of cultures from generation to generation.

Storytellers in indigenous cultures, such as Maori, usually stayed with their group, 'passing on the multiplicity of knowledge that any culture gathers and constructs about itself' (Bishop and Glynn, 1999). Westernised storytellers, such as travellers, troubadours and minstrels, moved from town to town conveying news through word, poetry and song (Parkin, 1998). Stories were exchanged around fires, in forests, on journeys, in village squares and inns and while waiting for catastrophes, such as plagues, to pass (Winter, Buck and Sobiechowska, 1999).

Travelling storytellers viewed their way of life as a vocation and the skills required to perform the role effectively were numerous. They included the ability to choose appropriate language, demonstrate insight and sensitivity and convey images that remained in the minds of listeners long after the storyteller had left the district. These same skills are required of storytellers today for we are, due to the specialisation of life in modern societies, all travellers in realms unknown to some of the people with whom we interact (Winter, Buck and Sobiechowska, 1999).

WHY ARE STORIES TOLD?

Winter, Buck and Sobiechowska (1999), although referring to written stories, offer insight into why many of us are fascinated with the narrative form. They suggest that by telling a story about a set of characters experiencing a particular series of events and working towards an acceptable outcome, we are in some ways exploring a theory. Like teaching, storytelling is a discursive process and an interpretive practice. As Pagano (1991: 197) contends, 'when we teach we tell stories about the world.

Some stories are scientific, some historical, some philosophical and so on'.

It makes sense then for educators to encourage students to tell stories about events they have experienced and to make links between stories of the world and their own stories. Witherell (1991: 84) explains: 'the creative use of story and dialogue lends power to educational and therapeutic experiences because of their capacity to expand our horizons of understanding and to provide rich contextual information about human actors, intentions, and experiences'. This capacity enables educators to use story and dialogue in various forms to help students make connections within and between self and other, subject and object, and thought and feeling.

To educate using storytelling is to take seriously the need for students to make sense of experience and seek meaning from their lives. Wells (1986: 194) sees it this way.

> Constructing stories in the mind – or storying as it has been called – is one of the most fundamental means of making meaning, as such, it is an activity that pervades all aspects of learning. When storying becomes overt and is given expression in word, the resulting stories are one of the most effective ways of making one's own interpretation of events and ideas available to others.

Acknowledging and sharing experiences and their contexts provides students with opportunities for reflective learning and the development of deeper relationships with others for 'we connect all of us, spaciously, timefully' (Keller, 1986: 248). If educators valued such connections and, when appropriate, taught using narrative modes of knowing, perhaps students would be better prepared to manage the challenges inherent in their personal and professional lives. Given that 'through knowledge and through our stories about our knowledge, we bring a sense of our own identify into focus' (Pagano, 1991: 199), storytelling is an ideal learning tool for expressing cultural realities, a view Bishop (1996) endorses.

Bishop and Glynn (1999) suggest the work of narrative therapists has valuable contributions to make to classroom practices because their approach encompasses the complexities of lives and relationships.

> The narratives we are talking about are the stories that people live. They are not 'about' life; they are life as we know it, life as we experience it. Since, as far as meaning, hope, fear, understanding, motivation, plans and the like are concerned, our life narratives are

our lives, it makes all the difference in the world what sort of narrative is available to a person (Freedman and Combs, 1996: 77).

Learning interactions within classrooms might also benefit if educators create opportunities for more complex, creative and diverse patterns of communication (Bishop and Glynn, 1999). Bishop (2001: 108) maintains 'we must attempt to create learning relationships within classrooms wherein learners' culturally generated sense-making processes are used and developed in order that they may successfully participate in classroom interaction'. Learning from this viewpoint is seen as the outcome of various interactions, which are co-created.

As a learning strategy, storytelling accommodates diverse realities and enables students to share experiences from their own cultural frame of reference (Bishop and Glynn, 1999). Viewed as an inclusive strategy, storytelling fulfills the needs of constructivists such as Lauritzen and Jaeger (1997) who recommend that educators take a narrative approach to curriculum development. Although a constructive approach may involve variable practices, it rests on a set of guiding principles. For Jonassen, Davidson, Collins, Campbell and Haag (1995) these principles are context, construction, collaboration and conversation. These principles are also conducive to narrative approaches to learning. Context, from this perspective, refers to the physical, cultural, social and political aspects embedded in stories and embodied in tellers and listeners, while the construction of knowledge is the result of their active participation in a storytelling process. Collaboration encompasses the relationships which develop between tellers and listeners and the ways in which they work together to construct new knowledge. Conversation is the means by which those involved articulate experience and engage in reflective dialogue.

The notion of viewing storytelling as a learning tool has appeal. Perhaps if we, as educators, were to describe storytelling as a process and view it 'as a way *to* knowing' in the same way Eraut (2000) suggests we think of intuition, we might advance our case for its widespread implementation in higher education contexts.

As a 'way *to* knowing' storytelling has the capacity to uncover, discover, freeze, create or re-imagine meaning and to enable the articulation of subsequent learning. By its very nature, patterns can be re-created, images portrayed and spaces made for the construction of knowledge. One of storytelling's strengths is its flexibility. We can work with stories or aspects of stories in many different ways; we can walk around them, wander through them, step into their centre or hover on the edge. Each approach enables us to relive, and come to know more fully, aspects of our experience. If we step back into our stories in some way, we have opportunities to, as Jung (1963) says, 'dream the dream on', and may eventually reach the point where we know, and can articulate, meaningful learning.

Bruner (1986: 69) stresses the importance of stories in understanding self and bringing cognition, emotion and action together to give experience 'cultural relevance'. Bishop and Glynn (1999: 177) maintain that 'stories are a powerful way of representing truth' for Maori and suggest 'different stories give different versions of and approaches to the truth'. The ability to accommodate multiple perspectives, along with ongoing transcultural usage, suggests that storytelling is a learning tool which can transcend cultural differences. It can also, on occasion, through performance, help us sense what narrative therapists refer to as that 'which is not yet known' (Freedman and Combs, 1996; Monk, Winslade, Crocket and Epston, 1997).

Indeed, Lopez (1987) reminds us that the most precious places in a culture are often invisible to the eye and contends that it is only through the drama of story (or dance or song) that they come into view. Individuals can also reveal their own invisible places through the stories they tell about themselves, their lives, and their experiences.

Storytelling enables us to impose meaning on chaotic experiences and, in the process, to find our own voice (Grumet, 1988). Stories also play a significant role in moral development (Tappan and Brown, 1991) and make accessible the themes of connection and care (Belenky, Clinchy, Goldberger and Tarule, 1986). Nurse educators, such as Benner (1984), contend that stories are a source of power and that sharing them often has a transformative effect on tellers and listeners.

Stories are also powerful research tools (Bishop, 1996; Josselson and Lieblich, 1995; McEwan and Egan, 1995; Witherell and Noddings, 1991). They enable us to enter into the worlds of real people involved in everyday situations. For a short time we get to imagine not only what the experiences being recalled might have felt like for the tellers but to consider how we would think, feel and act if faced with similar situations. In the process of engaging with stories, we construct meaning. Polkinghorne (1988: 6) says 'narrative meaning is created by noting that something is a "part" of a whole and that something is a "cause" of something else'. Stories allow us to glimpse the worlds of others and come to know our own world more fully.

Because stories hold educative and transformative possibilities they have significant roles to play in teaching and learning. As educators, we tell stories to students for many reasons: to introduce new material in entertaining and interesting ways, to share practice experiences which demonstrate key teaching points, and to reveal aspects of ourselves. We, the authors, also encourage students to tell stories about practice-related events. We use a narrative approach for three key reasons: first, to facilitate emotional release; second, to learn from experience; and third, to bring about thoughtful change to practice.

EMOTIONAL RELEASE

We have found that the most significant motivating force for students to tell stories comes from the emotions and feelings they experience while on clinical or work placements. These feelings and emotions often include powerlessness, embarrassment, anger, frustration, elation, pride, sadness and joy. The desire to release such affective responses provides students with the energy to seek out storytelling opportunities. When emotional release is the dominant motivating factor, the outcome is likely to be primarily cathartic.

Over time the need for catharsis may pass, or at least become less intense, although unresolved feelings from past experiences sometimes become tangled in present stories. This situation can result in students expressing intense feelings that seem out of proportion to those appropriate for their current story. When this happens, it is possible that unresolved issues from the past have become merged with current experiences and drive students' need for catharsis. Before such stories can be moved into the realm of learning through storytelling, past issues must be addressed.

Sometimes the process of telling a story once may be sufficient to enable students to move from being overwhelmed by affective components to a place where they can focus on gaining insight. On other occasions, students may need to tell their story many times to different people. Allowing time to pass between experiences, and telling stories about them, can also help integrate emotional reactions.

Another option for encouraging cathartic release is to identify recurring emotions within students' stories and to discuss how they might be managed within professional practice settings. Working in these ways can help bring about cathartic release and prepare students to learn from their stories.

LEARNING FROM EXPERIENCE

Although experience is sometimes described as though it were singular and not constrained by time and place, much of it is, as Boud, Cohen and

Walker (1993: 7) contend, 'multifaceted, multi-layered and so inextricably connected with other experiences, that it is impossible to locate temporally or spatially'. Therefore, attempting to recall, re-create and reflect on fleeting moments in order to learn from experience is a challenge. As Boud, Cohen and Walker's (1993) five propositions about learning from experience (as outlined in Chapter 2) suggest, learning is relational: it requires interaction, either directly or symbolically, with factors that are external to students. With storytelling, a key factor for tellers and listeners is dialogue.

Reason and Hawkins (1988) contend that the key to learning through storytelling is allowing meaning to develop through reflective dialogue. Dialogue ' is the moment where humans meet to reflect on their reality as they make it and remake it. It is the quintessential human act, the social moment wherein we establish ties, and where we have authentic recognition of the other' (Shor and Freire, 1987: 98–99). When we tell stories and process them, using reflective dialogue, we create the possibility for change in ourselves and in others. Our capacity to express ourselves through narrative forms not only enables us to reshape, reassess and reconstruct particular events, it allows us to learn from discussing our experiences with individuals who may raise alternative views, suggest imaginative possibilities and ask stimulating questions.

Brookfield and Preskill (1999) also support narrative forms of learning and advocate discussion as a way of teaching. They maintain that regardless of the term used – 'discussion', 'dialogue' or 'conversation' – students who are prepared to take a critical stance by engaging in lively interaction are committed to questioning and exploring diverse ideas and beliefs with open minds.

One indication of a liberating process is to encourage people to tell their stories critically (Freire, 1970). However, stories told in isolation and not reflectively processed are unlikely to lead to insight or result in meaningful learning. Another danger is when dialogue breaks down and meaning is imposed. Stories shift into becoming ideological tools rather than tools of discovery (Reason and Hawkins, 1988). If educators work with students to develop reflexive capability, this danger can be minimised.

Reflexive capability

Reflexive capacity develops when we engage in reflective dialogue (Brockbank and McGill, 1998), a view shared by Brookfield and Preskill (1999). Formalised storytelling processes provide students with such opportunities (Alterio, 1999a). Through dialogue, shaped to explore experiences in depth, multiple perspectives can emerge. From these perspectives, new learning and relationships can be constructed. As we establish these connections, part of the process of understanding past experiences may include re-imagining or reconstructing them, an approach used by narrative therapists such as White and Epston (1990).

Churchman (1971) concurs with Eckhartsberg's (1981) view that storytelling enables us to make multiple connections and reminds us that 'the underlying life of a story is its drama, not its accuracy' (p. 178). He views the best stories as those 'which stir people's minds, hearts and souls and by doing so give them new insights into themselves, their problems, and their human conditions' (p. 93). He sees a direct connection between storytelling and the construction of knowledge. Wilber (1981) agrees, and comments that 'meaning is established by unrestrained communicative inquiry and interpretation' (p. 32) and involves aspects of self-review.

Self-review

To increase the likelihood of gaining insight through storytelling, it is essential that students engage in forms of self-review. However, self-evaluative processes, by their very nature, can introduce a degree of vulnerability into the learning arena. As Nias and Groundwater (1988: 3) point out, 'to gather evidence about, to reflect upon and perhaps to change one's practice requires self-awareness, self-evaluation, self-revelation and probably creates self-doubt'. Yet these processes are necessary for on-going development. If we value the concept of development in its entirety, self-review, accompanied on occasions by discomfort, is an integral part of learning to be a professional.

Reflecting on personal experience to understand the nature and formation of self can reveal cultural–historical, individual–biographical, and interpersonal–relational patterns.

> It is our inward journey that leads us through time – forward or back, seldom in a straight line, most often spiralling. Each of us is moving, changing, with respect to others. As we discover, we remember, remembering, we discover; and most intensely do we experience this when our separate journeys converge (Welty, 1984: 102).

Building on Welty's work and on the writings of Dilthey (1977), Witherell (1991) draws our attention to the importance of developing 'an empathic understanding of human action through examining one's actions, intentions and history within the culture, language, and meaning systems in which one exists' (p. 90). Bruner (1983) cites the capacity for imaginative thinking and making use of help from others as key determinants for purposeful (reflective) learning. Others, such as Bruner (1986), Gilligan (1982) and Belenky *et al.* (1986), have stressed the value of subjective, imaginative and metaphorical ways of knowing.

These authors suggest, as Witherell (1991: 90) comments, that 'the self develops and finds meaning in the context of relationship – between self and other selves, subject and object, individual and culture, and between aspects of the self, both across and within the time dimension'. This view links with Vygotsky's (1987) socio-cultural theory in that it stresses the importance of connections and contexts in the development of self. As we have already stressed, one way to forge connections is through dialogue. We concur with Boud, Cohen and Walker (1993: 19) who contend that 'to enter into dialogue with our own biographies as learners is a helpful means to reflect on and reframe our practice'. Through dialogue we increase our knowledge of self and strengthen our connections with others. Dialogue that encourages reflection creates spaces in which it is possible to construct meaning and explore the skills and knowledge that underpin practice, thereby validating experience and opening up the possibility for change.

BRINGING ABOUT CHANGE TO PRACTICE

Potential for change is always present. However, altering the way we view ourselves and aspects of our professional lives can be unsettling because, for change to occur, our 'existing network of concepts has to be broken down to some extent in order to be reformed and developed' (Harrison, 1962, cited by Dadds, 1993: 288). Also, as changed perspectives increase self-knowledge, insight into personal and professional situations and relationships may follow and necessitate further actions. Therefore, when students in higher education contexts learn through storytelling, it is prudent for educators to have a range of support strategies in place. Such strategies might include peer-support initiatives, access to student counsellors and regular small group meetings between students and educators. It is also helpful if educators assist students to develop an appreciation of what is involved when stories are told.

When we encourage students to participate in self-review activities we risk introducing an element of vulnerability into the learning arena. If students are aware that feeling uncomfortable on occasions can be expected and indeed is integral to the learning process, they can manage these times more constructively. When students understand this and remain open to creative possibilities, they are more likely to recognise the need to bring about changes to practice and to implement them in thoughtful and safe ways.

It is also highly possible, within learning contexts, that storytelling processes, which incorporate reflective dialogue, contribute to the development of professional knowledge and affect our sense of self and our relationships. To understand better how telling and processing stories might influence relationships, it is useful to explore the role of emotion, an area which until recently received scant attention from educators.

Emotional realities

Revealing emotional aspects and valuing them as integral to experience enriches storytelling processes. However, we often feel more than we can easily express. Feeling, according to Mulligan (1993), is one of two major ways in which we make judgements about the world, the other being reasoning (thinking). What we feel accentuates that which is subjectively important to us and reveals our likes and dislikes, our values and preferences, while what we think tends to be based on theories, frameworks and concepts and is, therefore, more objective.

To maximise learning gains through storytelling we need to incorporate both subjective and objective perspectives. However, not all educators are willing to incorporate emotion in their teaching. Research on the paradox of emotion and educational leadership highlights how emotion is frequently viewed and educator–student relationships often managed (Beatty, 2000). Teachers and educational leaders told Beatty (2000) that being an educator involved a tremendous amount of emotion; however, she found that 'in current practice, the emotionality of teaching and learning is often, largely, a matter of emotional control' (p. 2). Given this finding, she urges educators to embrace and use the emotional realities of their lives as teachers rather than perpetuate the long-standing practice of emotional avoidance within educational environments.

For such a shift to occur, Beatty (2000: 7) contends that educators need to 'acknowledge relationship and real relationship requires authenticity' which involves time and energy, commodities already in short supply in education contexts. As a consequence educators often 'manage' aspects of their roles in isolation and keep their emotions under control, settling for what Hargeaves (1994) calls 'contrived collegiality' (cited by Beatty, 2000: 8). If meaningful relationships with colleagues are impersonal, educators are unlikely to establish authentic relationships with students unless they are integrated into the learning process. Authentic relationships involve trust and collaboration, both fundamentally emotional and, we believe, essential aspects of storytelling.

When educators and students work with stories, emotional responses can be managed in appropriate and meaningful ways by using formal processes. Through the process of telling stories we have opportunities to join the worlds of thought and feeling (Brody, Witherell, McDonald and Lundblad, 1991). The inclusion of feelings is fundamental to human experience and can no longer be ignored in education sectors. After all, teaching and learning are profoundly emotional activities (Fried, 1995).

In their model of reflection in the learning process, Boud, Keogh and Walker (1985) attend to feelings in two ways: first, by working with positive feelings and second, by removing obstructive feelings. They maintain that one gain that results from working with positive feelings is the potential it provides for students to anticipate the possible benefits they may accrue by processing their experiences. Likewise, if students are assisted to deal with obstructive feelings associated with their experiences they are more likely to engage in rationale processing (Boud, Keogh and Walker, 1985). Often some form of catharsis will remove obstructive feelings and it is this release that sometimes generates spontaneous insights into their origins and effects (Heron, 1979). Storytelling processes that involve reflective dialogue also aid catharsis. However, their greatest potential is in the facilitation of learning, learning which has the potential to bring about thoughtful change to self and practice. In the next chapter we offer some ideas on how we think learning through storytelling might be managed within a theoretical framework.

4 Storytelling as a Theory of Learning

In this chapter we take a fourfold approach to the question 'How are stories told?'. We begin with a brief exploration of how storytelling approaches become aligned to particular paradigms. After positioning our work within a socio-cultural framework, and justifying our reasons for doing so, we present a theoretical model to demonstrate how we think learning through storytelling, using our approach, occurs. We then introduce a Storytelling Pathways Model to highlight how students can consciously choose processes that enable them to achieve different learning outcomes. Finally, we present our Reflective Learning through Storytelling Model.

POSITIONING STORYTELLING

We generally know what paradigm educators are working in by the language they use and the learning and teaching principles they espouse and strive to uphold. To explore what paradigm-related observations educators have made about the positioning of storytelling we return to the literature. While many educators accept there is a world-view that admits story as a way of knowing, paradigmatical allegiances are less clear. We wonder if this is because there is confusion over where story fits, due to the nature of the learning tool itself, or because there are difficulties inherent in the notion of paradigms. Such questions continue to intrigue us. While the latter is beyond the scope of this book, the former warrants attention, for, in the process of writing this book we had to declare which paradigm most supported our current way of working with stories. Making this decision was not straightforward because narrative is used and sits comfortably within a number of paradigms such as constructivist (Lauritzen and Jaeger, 1997) and hermeneutics (Josselson and Lieblich, 1995; McEwan, 1995; Polkinghorne, 1988). In New Zealand, educators such as Bishop (2001) currently advocate a constructivist approach, given its ability to accommodate 'learners' culturally generated sense-making processes' (p. 108). It is also worth noting that within cultures there are ideological and other related interests that impact on the ways in which we construct knowledge.

While constructivism stands alone for some authors, for others it sits within an interpretive framework in which meaning and understanding is emphasised (Greene, 1996; Fosnot, 1996). It can also be viewed as a psychological theory, with application to adult education practices, for constructivism focuses on knowledge and the way it is constructed (Arlidge, 2000). Educators working within constructivist frameworks believe 'that learning is a process of sense-making, of adding and synthesising new information within existing knowledge structures' (Arlidge, 2000: 34). Chaille and Britain (1991: 11) describe it this way:

> The learner is actively constructing knowledge rather than passively taking in information. Learners come to the educational setting with many different experiences, ideas, and approaches to learning. Learners do not *acquire* knowledge that is transmitted to them; rather, they *construct* knowledge through their intellectual activity and make it their own.

The language used in this text, and the tenets that underpin our storytelling processes (context, collaboration, conversation and construct), together with our Vygotskian links, suggest we are currently positioned within a constructivist framework. There are, however, two strands of constructivism: psychological/cognitive constructivism and socio-cultural and social constructivism. While differences between the two perspectives are not always clear, nor unproblematic (Arlidge, 2000), since both share commonalities such as students being actively involved in the learning process, it is worth taking a moment to establish on which side of the constructivist coin we are positioned.

The literature suggests that educators working within psychological constructivism tend to focus on the way students construct knowledge, while socio-cultural constructivists such as Vygotsky are more concerned with communication processes and the influence of social factors on the construction of knowledge (Philips, 1997a, 1997b). Vygotsky emphasises the importance of language and dialogue, the social contexts of learning in the construction of knowledge (Wilson, Teslow and Taylor, 1993), and the students' unassisted and assisted capabilities (zone of proximal development). He also recognises the importance of 'culturally situated learning, believing that educational interactions reflect the surrounding culture' (Vygotsky, cited by Arlidge, 2000: 37).

Our storytelling approach has allegiances with Vygotskyian perspectives because we view learning as a social and collaborative process that values students' prior knowledge and experience and promotes reflective dialogue as a medium through which knowledge can be constructed. We also acknowledge that while we construct our worlds, we do so in interaction with social, historical, ideological and cultural contexts. In fact we influence and, in turn, are influenced by these contexts.

By positioning our work within a socio-cultural framework we are acknowledging that ways of talking are central to the learning process (Shotter, 1995), and these encounters are influenced by cultural contexts. We also hold the view that construction is more than a simple contextual matter; it is a process, and very much a complex issue of influences that include the role of discourse.

Learning processes that promote dialogue are central to effective storytelling approaches. So, too, are meaning-making and reflective processes. As we developed our thoughts on how learning occurs when storytelling is used as the primary tool, we found Entwistle's (1996) work with surface and deep learning, and Moon's (1999) five-stage Map of Learning particularly useful. An overview of Moon's (1999, 2001) work, which incorporates Entwistle's concepts of surface and deep learning, follows.

STAGES OF LEARNING

Noticing

Noticing how we perceive what is around us is the first stage in Moon's (1999) Map of Learning. This stage is influenced by various factors, four of which are what students already know, what they imagine the purpose of learning to be, what emotional responses are evoked by the learning situation, and how the material to be learned is presented to them. Noticing something does not mean learning will occur, for students at this stage are functioning at a surface level.

Making sense

Characterised by surface approaches to learning, students operating at this stage are concerned with the learning material itself and not with links it may have to prior knowledge and experience. The primary focus is on organising and ordering the material of learning and putting ideas together. Any integration of learning material will be at a superficial level.

Making meaning

At this stage students assimilate new material into their cognitive structure and, at the same time, the cognitive structure accommodates this material to make sense of their new learning in relation to what they already know. As a result, meaningful learning and understanding occurs and, on occasions, students may experience a sense of emotional 'rightness' (Entwistle, 1996; Head and Sutton, 1985). When learning gains are maximised during this stage 'deep learning with the ideas being linked together and evidence of a holistic view of the subject matter' (Moon, 1999: 143) are demonstrated.

Working with meaning

The focus shifts in this stage from original material of learning, which may have been modified in the process of accommodation, and moves to ideas generated as a result of ongoing learning. Students are likely to engage in forms of reflection. Thoughts may be clarified, problem-solving strategies implemented and judgements made. Students may engage in review processes, which raises their awareness of the ways in which personal knowledge influences actions taken in professional practice contexts.

Transformative learning

Learning at this stage involves a more sophisticated and comprehensive accommodation of the cognitive structure. Students demonstrate the ability to evaluate their own frames of reference and convey an understanding of their own and other people's knowledge. Such awareness of the learning process itself enables students to take a critical overview of their own and others' knowledge. Students are self-motivated and self-motivating, able to engage constructively in thoughtful and reasoned discussions and make judgements about the usefulness of material and ideas from a range of sources.

These five stages mirror, in many ways, how we work with students and their stories, a discovery which prompted us to develop, in a formal sense, a Reflective Learning through Storytelling Model. Before we present this model (Figure 5, p. 60) we demonstrate our initial links with Moon's (1999) Map of Learning in Table 1.

Table 1: Links between Learning and Storytelling

Map of Learning (Moon, 1999)	Learning through Storytelling
• Noticing • Making sense • Making meaning • Working with meaning • Transformative learning	• Story finding • Story telling • Story expanding • Story processing • Story reconstructing

REFLECTIVE LEARNING THROUGH STORYTELLING

When we use storytelling as a learning tool, students' past experiences, attitudes towards storytelling and intensity of feelings engendered by particular stories, together with how these stories are processed, influence how and what is learned. While storytelling is reliant on both tellers and listeners, it is fundamental to appreciate that every story is presented from the teller's perspective. Motives, ideas, words or events depict their point of view and are substantiated through tone of voice, points of emphasis and gestures. Tellers choose which elements will be included and excluded and how they present their stories. Tellers also determine what level of affective involvement they will reveal.

Stories that appeal to some students may have little relevance to others given that our sense-making processes are culturally generated. While some stories evoke powerful cathartic responses, others may cause little, if any, emotional connection. The stories students tend to find appealing and want to tell, or listen to, are often those that connect in some way with their own experiences. These connections may be thematic, social, cultural or perhaps relate to current interests. For example, a student teacher might tell a story about a classroom interaction that intrigued or concerned her.

Like Moon (1999) we found, by taking a five-stage approach to learning, we were able to work with students and their stories in meaningful ways. The stages of our Reflective Learning through Storytelling Model are now outlined.

Story finding

The stories we find, and have an urgent need to tell, are frequently high in emotional content. Something about a situation excites, upsets or intrigues us. We may be overwhelmed by emotions and not always aware of why we are thinking about a particular situation. In one of our storytelling sessions a teller, when asked why he had told a particular story, said, 'I don't know, it just found me'. This is a common response during this first stage.

Story telling

In the second stage, tellers and listeners focus on organising and ordering content. Stories are told and listened to for the purpose of understanding the story itself. Students attempt to make sense both of context and of human experience (Josselson, 1995). There may be some linking of ideas; however, this tends to be at a surface level. Tellers and listeners are more interested in making sense of the story that is being presented although, at this stage, relationships between listeners and tellers are in the process of being established.

Story expanding

This stage is characterised by making meaning of the events being shared. Throughout the storytelling process forgotten aspects are frequently recalled, which sometimes necessitates a degree of backtracking. Questions are asked, important aspects expanded on and feelings clarified. Tellers and listeners who are actively and reflectively engaged in the process assimilate new learning into their cognitive structures which concurrently accommodates it and enables links to be made with existing knowledge and past experience. Past experience may include how often aspects of the situation being described have happened to tellers and how aware they are of any connections. The intensity of feelings associated with particular stories may indicate the presence of unresolved emotions from prior situations that are similar in some way to those being recalled, and this relationship can affect learning potential for some tellers. This is also true for listeners who have experienced similar situations.

Crucial to the successful presentation of any story is how the question 'Why?' is addressed. Why did events unfold in particular ways and why did key players behave in certain ways?

When meaningful and reasoned connections are made and there is evidence of an holistic approach to shared events, a shift from surface to deep learning takes place.

Story processing

Deep learning is associated with reflective activity, a key aspect of this stage where the focus shifts to working with meaning and, in particular, developing, through reflective dialogue, multiple perspectives of events. Tellers and listeners engage in review processes that raise awareness of how personal knowledge influences actions taken in professional practice contexts. Tellers' feelings are acknowledged and valued. Possible resolutions or solutions to unresolved situations are formulated.

To some degree, the listeners' understanding and their experiences of the situations that are being related shape this stage. The ways in which listeners engage tellers in reflective questioning influences what they themselves learn. While listeners can gain insight through dialogue, tellers have opportunities to challenge listeners' interpretation of events. Thus, tellers retain control of their stories and can confirm, elaborate, explain, clarify or refute aspects raised by listeners. At the same time issues can be critically explored, resulting in a deeper understanding of the significance of particular stories and the interrelationships between meaning and context.

This stage frequently calls forth aspects that have been forgotten, and can bring to the surface other stories that are connected in some way to present situations. Reflectively processing these connections so links are made between present situations and past experiences, and being open to alternative perspectives, enables tellers to move to the fifth stage which has a critical emphasis.

Story reconstructing

In this final stage, tellers and listeners demonstrate an ability to interrogate stories critically from as many perspectives as possible. They also critically evaluate the potential of resolutions and solutions (Kemmis, 1985; Taylor, 1998). Implications to self and practice are considered as each resolution or solution is evaluated. Dialogue is reasoned, thoughtful and constructive. Tellers and listeners are more aware of what has shaped their perspectives. Stories are reconstructed and, in the process, there is the potential for those involved to be 'transformed, transfigured and transported by stories' (Jackson, 1995: 12). This stage offers opportunities for tellers and listeners to bring about change to practice.

Gudmundsdottir (1995: 34) agrees that 'narratives are valuable *transformation* tools' and goes on to say that in most instances:

> . . . transformations mean progressing from an incomplete story to one that is more complete and compelling. We do this by establishing first the connectedness or coherence that moves the storyline along through time. Next comes the direction of the story, the goal or the point of it

all. With the goal established, events are selected, rejected, or transformed and take on a significance that they would not have otherwise possessed.

Some stories change us in ways that have little to do with knowledge and more to do with ways of being. When stories touch us in this manner, the way we view others and ourselves and the worlds we inhabit alters irrevocably. 'We become acquainted with aspects of life that have been previously unknown. In short, they *transform* us, alter us as individuals' (Jackson, 1995: 9).

However, these gains do not always occur. Some stories are told and retold without any obvious sense of advancement or resolution. Questions are left unanswered or conflicts and concerns unresolved. As a result, learning opportunities are missed. Therefore, it is useful to explore how storytelling can lead to the richest gains. If, as Josselson (1995: 35) contends, 'narrative models of knowing are models of process *in process*', we need to consider how we tell stories.

HOW ARE STORIES TOLD?

Educators encourage students to tell practice-related stories for many reasons. They also use a variety of approaches to facilitate the telling and exploration of student stories. We discovered that how students told and processed their stories determined what learning outcomes they could achieve, an observation that led to the development of a storytelling pathways model (McDrury and Alterio, 2001). Using this model, we were able to demonstrate how students could achieve different learning outcomes by mixing three key factors: setting, type of story and number of listeners. These factors are clustered into three key storytelling characteristics:

1.   *Setting* – is it informal or formal?
2.   *Listeners* – is there one or are there many?
3.   *Story* – is it spontaneous or pre-determined?

Each characteristic contributes to the storytelling process in a unique way.

Setting

We note that there are two settings. *Happening settings*, where events take place, and *telling settings*, where stories are told about these events.

We acknowledge that time differences between events occurring and stories being told about them will vary, and that these variations may influence how and why stories are told. We also believe that learning outcomes are dependent on the type of interaction different settings accommodate, a view we now substantiate.

Telling settings, where stories are shared, may be informal or formal. Informal settings allow for casual encounters while formal settings require planning and negotiation. Informal storytelling occurs when there is a story to tell, a willing listener or listeners, and a suitable physical space. Meal breaks are frequently used as they provide brief opportunities to share dramas as they unfold. However, this form of storytelling is by no means limited to canteens and cafeterias. Brief meetings in corridors, stairwells or other liminal spaces are also used.

Taking an informal pathway means that tellers and listeners construct the storytelling process as it evolves. When tellers have strong cathartic needs, dialogue on story content is less likely to occur, limiting opportunities for learning. Another factor that impacts on learning potential relates to how listeners respond to tellers' stories. In informal settings, responses tend to be variable and frequently result in listeners sharing their own stories. These stories often mirror the feelings and intensity that have been revealed in the tellers' stories. While there may be cathartic release, significant learning is unlikely.

To increase the likelihood of learning from stories, it is necessary to move beyond the casual exchange of experience and focus more particularly on the learning process by placing storytelling in formal settings. Availability for such opportunities varies. Currently there are notable differences in the way educators use storytelling. It is still perceived as 'professional gossip' in some groups (Laing, 1993), while we, by formalising the process, have elevated it to an integral part of professional development (Alterio, 1999b; McDrury and Alterio, 2001). Formal storytelling is conducive to promoting dialogue, valuing affective responses and providing opportunities to explore alternative approaches to practice dilemmas. Listeners play a key role in these processes.

Listeners

Listeners help shape the storytelling process and influence outcomes by listening to stories and engaging tellers in reflective dialogue. Listeners can play a notable role during dialogue by influencing, through reflective questioning and other strategies, the level, breadth and degree of reflection that takes place. In all five stages of our storytelling model, listeners are co-learners who can benefit from being part of the process. Learning may occur for listeners in multifaceted forms: through involvement in various storytelling processes; through listening to tellers' accounts of experiences that they too may have encountered, in their entirety or in part; and by engaging in reflective discussions. As stories are processed, those present frequently realise that their individual experiences are collectively experienced predicaments. While the details and key players may differ, the difficulties encountered are essentially the same (Brookfield, 1995). Therefore significant learning can occur for both tellers and listeners. In our experience such learning is most likely to occur during the processing stage, which frequently involves some form of dialogue.

Dialogue occurs in two key ways: *response discourse* and *response story*. If listeners remain focused on the original story, dialogue centres on elements of the practice experience being related. When this happens listeners engage in what we term *response discourse*, which helps the teller explore their experience in depth. If listeners react by telling what we call a *response story*, dialogue shifts to include this experience. While the response story may pick up a theme from the original story by exploring a similar event, some *response stories* are only loosely connected to the original theme and can thereby shift the focus considerably. We use the term *story hijacking* to convey the sense of outrage some students feel when this occurs. Maria, a second-year Business Administration student, explains:

> Over lunch I was telling a small group of classmates about a terrible work placement I'd recently experienced. It had really unsettled me and I needed them to listen, perhaps support me. I was thinking that maybe I wasn't suited to office work. I'd hardly begun when one of my classmates butted in and told a story about her experience. It was about the same kind of thing, being treated like everyone's slave but not being shown how to do anything so of course, you do everything wrong. Then someone else jumped in with something that happened to her when she had a holiday job in an office and before I knew it they were telling each other about the part-time jobs they'd had at high school. I felt frustrated even though some of the stories were very funny. I remember walking away feeling quite upset because I hadn't been listened to and I hadn't worked out how to make my next placement a better experience.

Maria shared her story-hijacking experience during a session on listening to, focusing on and staying with one story. In the discussion that ensued, every student in the class was able to recall several occasions where they had experienced similar feelings of frustration when a story they considered important was hijacked. In every instance, these stories were told in informal settings such as inside a car, in a café, at a party or a family gathering.

We think response stories are more likely to occur in informal settings because of the casual, spontaneous and evolving nature of the storytelling process. If tellers wish to engage in meaningful learning, an added dimension must be incorporated. It is sometimes enough for tellers to finish a story by asking specific questions such as 'What would you do in this situation?' or 'How could I have dealt with this differently?'. Using these questions, tellers can attempt to contain or direct replies towards a response discourse. However, in informal settings, listeners may ignore such prompts and still recount their own response stories.

In formal settings, processes can be put in place to minimise the occurrence of response stories and maximise dialogue focused on the primary story. When one listener and one teller dialogue on story content in a formal setting designed to facilitate reflective learning, they are more likely to uncover layers of meaning which focus on the teller's perspective, although the listener may contribute an added dimension. It is also possible that solutions or strategies may be generated when dialogue remains focused. Terry, a third-year social work student, explains:

> I thought I'd cracked it, this thing I've got with names and faces. You'd think I'd be good at it because it goes with the job but I really have a problem. It's something I have to work at. Then I thought I had a breakthrough. I was at a funeral, a mate's, when I saw someone I recognised coming up the steps. I couldn't remember his name but I knew the face. I went up to him and asked how his work was going, he did the same then we said something about the funeral before going into the church. I felt really chuffed. I told my family about it later the same night. I was still trying to remember his name when you wouldn't believe it. There he was on the TV screen. He's a newsreader I see most nights. So here I am back to square one.

This story was told to one listener, another student, in a formal setting, a classroom in a higher education institution. While laughter followed the telling and brief accounts of other embarrassing moments were shared, the listener and teller quickly moved into dialogue centred on how Terry might overcome his difficulty remembering names. The process, while initially cathartic, moved to the formulation of several strategies that Terry could implement. He found one strategy effective: visualising the person's name as a story title, for example 'TERRY FRASER', then coming up with a characteristic which described the person using the first letters of their name, for example 'Talks Fast'. After the storytelling session Terry remarked that not only did he feel better for having revealed his difficulty, but he now felt he had a strategy to help him improve his ability to recall and retain names.

When several listeners view a story from multiple perspectives, they further increase the opportunity to uncover new and possibly totally unexpected learning. Sue, a woman who had returned to the workforce after raising a family, recalled an experience she said nearly ended her paid working life.

> I was training to be a caregiver. As part of my course I had to work one day a week in a Rest Home for the confused elderly. I thought it would be pretty cruisey, lots of sitting around drinking cups of tea and chatting. Actually it turned out to be hard work. One of my duties was to toilet everyone on a rotating basis whether they wanted to go or not. It was a dreadful task because sometimes they didn't want to come with me, other times, if they couldn't go, I turned the tap on to help them. One day, I'll never forget it. I was feeling cranky because everyone was being difficult. I finally got round to an old chap who was sitting in a chair. He didn't want to come with me. He kept telling me he wanted to go home. They all say that. I finally got him into the toilet but he refused to take down his trousers no matter what I said so I tried to undo his fly myself. There he was saying he didn't want to go when my supervisor came in to see what all the noise was about. She asked me what I was doing. I told her I was trying to toilet him. That's when she told me he was a visitor, not a resident.

Sue told this story to a small group of listeners in a formal setting, a classroom in a higher education institution. Once again the initial response was cathartic and expressed through laughter. Because Sue desperately wanted to understand why she had failed to distinguish between a resident and a visitor, once the laughter had subsided she asked her listeners a series of questions, including 'What can I do to ensure this never happens again?'. This approach kept the focus on Sue's dilemma and resulted in a number of suggestions. The strategy she found most helpful came from a student who 'wondered' if she could ask a staff member, before commencing work, who she was responsible for and how she might identify them.

In these three story examples, students revealed how making a mistake had shaken their confidence to perform an aspect of their work. Maria, who told her story in an informal setting, fared less well than Terry and Sue whose stories were shared in formal settings, demonstrating that where we tell stories influences how they are received and processed. The type of story we tell also affects how and what we might learn from experience.

Story

Stories tend to have spontaneous origins and occur primarily because tellers need to share particular events or situations that lend themselves to such tellings. *Spontaneous storytelling*, closely linked in time to practice settings, frequently has a strong affective motivating force. The details are crafted around this need and elements are emphasised and minimised to ensure that the dramas of stories are shared through the tellings.

Less common, but more likely to result in reflective learning, is *predetermined storytelling* where the teller has considered the event in a pre-story reflective phase and wants to explore it further. Any additional work will, therefore, build on insights already gained. When such storytelling takes place in an informal setting, the teller frequently wants dialogue in the form of a response discourse. However, the reality is that listeners often tell a response story. It is only in a formal setting that response discourse can be assured.

Regardless of the setting, it is by no means clear which parts of an experience will be shared. Certainly there are some experiences which do not receive a 'second thought' because they do not engage the student in either 'reflection-in-action' or 'reflection-on-action' (Schön, 1983, 1987). Unless there is a trigger event such as someone sharing an experience that is in some way linked, these stories remain unexamined.

In contrast, there are stories that cause the teller to ponder the event either during or after the experience. Sometimes it is simple curiosity that leads to a telling, but on other occasions there may be unanswered questions relating to knowledge and skills, or involving interpersonal dynamics. There are also occasions when the impact of an experience moves beyond a surface involvement and touches a deeper space inside the teller where there is a particular level of openness and vulnerability. Sharing these stories is usually carefully planned because they are almost unspeakable and, therefore, particularly suited to formal settings.

Some stories are re-told many times to different listeners for a variety of reasons. Events that are significant for tellers are more likely to be re-told in an attempt to explore them in depth and thus make meaning from experience. With each re-telling, new learning can occur. This is particularly likely when tellers make conscious choices about how they tell their stories.

STORYTELLING PATHWAYS

The setting, number of listeners and type of story are three areas of choice available to tellers. The pathways taken determine the level of catharsis and reflective learning which can be achieved. When students understand the consequences of using different pathways, their reflective learning potential is enhanced. Students may choose to re-tell particular stories using different pathways to attain different learning outcomes. These pathways are now described and presented diagrammatically (Figures 1, 2, 3 and 4).

Informal setting, single listener

Pathway 1, the *informal setting, single listener, spontaneous story* is likely to achieve the greatest level of catharsis. One listener can provide undivided attention to the teller and is more likely to focus on the affective domain. This pathway may also provide greater freedom for the teller to express unedited ideas, concerns and feelings.

Pathway 2, the *informal setting, single listener, predetermined story* is still likely to contain a strong affective element. It also involves an initial reflective phase prior to the telling, when the teller decides which story to share. This phase helps focus the teller on the experience. If time allows for post-story discussion, the listener is more likely to pick up on the teller's concerns, uncertainties or needs and ask associated questions.

Figure 1:   Pathways 1 & 2

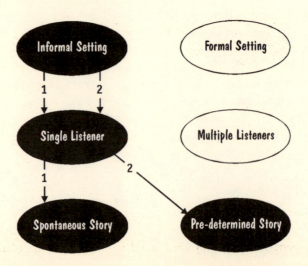

Informal setting, multiple listeners

Pathway 3, the *informal setting, multiple listeners, spontaneous story* is likely to be dominated by various listeners sharing their experiences, resulting in the teller's story being hijacked. What the teller shares may become fragmented as listeners interject with stories about their own experiences. Some of these stories may also be told in parts. Sharing multiple story fragments can lead to a joint catharsis.

Pathway 4, the *informal setting, multiple listeners, predetermined story* is likely to result in dialogue that focuses on the practice event. Absence of a formal setting and a structured process can, however, minimise the effectiveness of discussion and shift the focus away from the teller's needs.

Figure 2:   Pathways 3 & 4

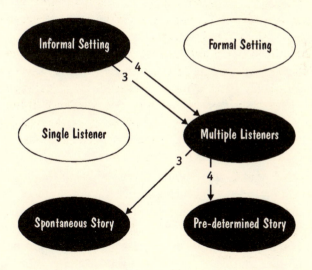

Formal setting, single listener

Pathway 5, the *formal setting, single listener, spontaneous story* provides an opportunity for the teller and listener to enter into dialogue which is focused and fruitful because of an agreed agenda. Both partners in the reflective process have responsibilities. The teller's responsibility is to share the story and be willing to explore its meaning; the listener's responsibility is to construct appropriate questions or responses to encourage reflection.

Pathway 6, the *formal setting, single listener, predetermined story* has all the benefits of Pathway 5 and has the added advantage of an initial reflective phase. This phase requires the teller to decide which story to share and may involve judgements on aspects such as appropriateness and implications.

Figure 3:   Pathways 5 & 6

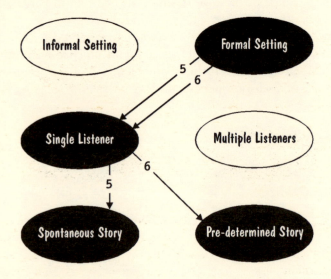

Formal setting, multiple listeners

Pathway 7, the *formal setting, multiple listeners, spontaneous story* involves a reflective group process in which a story is shared, a practice situation examined and alternative approaches explored. With a number of listeners there are opportunities to clarify the teller's understanding of the story and explore multiple perspectives. With this additional information the teller can consider alternative actions and evaluate possible consequences.

Pathway 8, the *formal setting, multiple listeners, predetermined story* means the teller has considered the event prior to the storytelling process. This prior reflection enhances the gains outlined in Pathway 7, and is likely to result in significant learning.

These eight pathways represent options that are available to tellers and there may well be others. While each of the pathways we have presented has a unique role, we stress that there will be times when one-to-one story-telling processes feel more appropriate than group storytelling and vice versa. There will also be occasions when informal settings better suit particular storytelling moments than formal ones. Likewise, there will

Figure 4:   Pathways 7 & 8

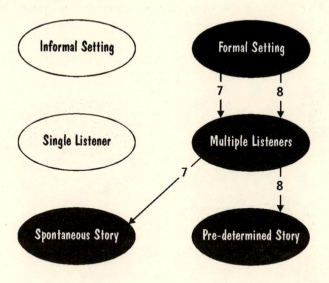

always be a place for both spontaneous and predetermined stories.

How we tell stories, where we tell them and what type of stories we share are as changeable as the stories themselves. Storytelling is, and will always be, a multipurposed, multifaceted and multilayered human resource each of us carries within us and uses in various ways throughout our lives. As journalist Robert Fulford (2000) observes, stories 'are the juncture where facts and feelings meet' (p. 9).

Our interest, from an educative perspective, lies with how storytelling can be used to bring about learning related to the development of professional practice. We contend that reflective learning and the ability to bring about thoughtful and reasoned change to practice is more likely to occur when tellers and listeners work collaboratively in formal contexts to construct knowledge using processes which promote reflective dialogue. The following model (Figure 5) draws together the ideas presented in this chapter.

While conscious selection of storytelling characteristics and motivations to achieve particular outcomes enables students to maximise learning gains, what tellers and listeners learn from participating in the same storytelling process may differ. What they bring to and take away from storytelling is dependent on many factors, one being how it is introduced as a learning tool and how associated processes are managed. In the next chapter we outline how a storytelling culture can be established and provide a range of activities educators can use to assist students with the *story finding* stage of our model.

Figure 5: Model of Reflective Learning through Storytelling

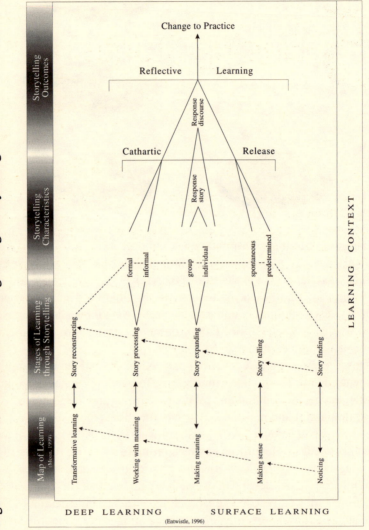

Figure 5: Model of Reflective Learning through Storytelling

5 Finding Stories

It is one thing to recognise storytelling's potential as a reflective learning tool. It is another thing to use it confidently. While some educators and students will find stories spontaneously, others may take time to feel comfortable working with them. In this chapter we offer some activities that can be used to establish the beginnings of a storytelling culture. These activities come from a variety of sources and have been adapted to suit our purposes. Where possible we acknowledge their source or, if the source is unknown, we thank the individuals who introduced them to us. Some activities were generated as we taught or worked in clinical settings. A few arrived unannounced in the middle of the night. Several have their origins in creative writing or drama workshops. Most have been used many times with many groups. As with all teaching and learning resources, their appeal will vary. We hope, by offering a range of activities, that educators and students will find several to entice them into the realm of storytelling. Before each activity is described, general information is provided under the headings purpose, group size, time and resources.

CREATING A STORYTELLING CULTURE

We suggest these storytelling activities be held, where possible, in comfortable venues with space to break into small groups. The activities we describe are not presented in any order nor are they sacrosanct. It is up to educators and students to decide which activities to use and how to adapt them to meet specific learning needs. We do suggest, however, that educators attend to confidentiality matters with students and ensure that appropriate support is provided. For detailed accounts of how we manage these aspects when using formalised storytelling processes, we direct readers to Chapters 8 and 9. In Chapter 10 we address ethical dilemmas from a general perspective. Storytellers may wish to familiarise themselves with this content prior to using the activities outlined in this chapter.

Our personal and professional experiences influence how we use storytelling as a learning tool. As demonstrated in our own stories, some of us connect more easily with the oral tradition while others have a strong affinity with the written form. With this difference in mind, we offer a mix of oral and written activities.

STORYTELLING ACTIVITIES

▲ Stories and places

Purpose: To highlight everyday usage of storytelling.
Group size: This activity works equally well with small and large groups.
Time: 10 minutes for 10–12 students, longer for a larger group.
Resources: Whiteboard, whiteboard pens.

The educator asks students to form pairs, and to think about, and record, where they have encountered stories in the previous 24 hours. Examples include books, movies, newspapers, television, friends, family, Internet, shops, buses, phone, canteens, classrooms, sportsfields, restaurants, cafés and barbecues. Each pair reports back to the main group. The educator may wish to depict storytelling's popularity as a sun diagram on the whiteboard (see Figure 6).

Figure 6:   Story Sun Diagram

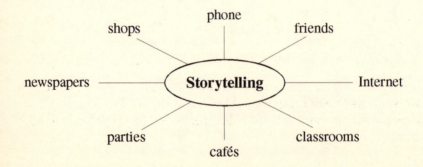

▲ *Making connections*

Purpose: To make connections and establish prior learning.
Size: This exercise works equally well with small and large groups.
Time: 15 minutes for 10–12 students, longer for a larger group.
Resources: One Index card for each student headed 'Story Forms', whiteboard and whiteboard pens or an overhead projector and transparency.

The educator introduces the topic of 'different story forms' and hands each student an index card. Students are asked to move around the room engaging each other in brief discussions about story forms. Each person is required to gather five story forms, for example myth, legend, fairytale, biography, memoir, fictional and media-related, which they must record on their card and have the contributor sign.

Once everyone has gathered this information, it is shared in the large group and written on a whiteboard or overhead transparency. While the interaction encourages connection, the display enables the educator to take into account what the group already knows about the topic.

▲ *Word associations*

Purpose: To encourage spontaneity and creativity.
Group size: This exercise works equally well with small and large groups.
Time: 20 minutes for 10–12 students, longer for a larger group.
Resources: Paper and pens, and a list of words about a specific topic, for example:

Professional Practice
- •   Reflection
- •   Ethics
- •   Praxis
- •   Cultural Safety.

Activity 1

The educator reads each word or phrase in turn, allowing time in between for students to write responses. Responses may take various forms, for example an emotion, a definition, an experience, a line of poetry or a single word.

Activity 2
Students, in pairs, tell each other a real or imagined story about a situation using at least two of their response words or phrases.

▲ *Statements and responses*

Purpose: To elicit quick responses to a topic, e.g. self-review.
Group size: This exercise works equally well with small and large groups.
Time: 20 minutes for 10–12 students, longer for a larger group.
Resources: An A4 sheet of paper with a statement and response box for
                   each student as depicted below, and pens.

Statement
Telling stories about our personal and professional lives can be a revealing and often disconcerting experience because we are exploring the very images we hold of ourselves as practitioners (Alterio, 1998).

Response

After introducing the concept of self-review, the educator hands out the A4 sheets and asks each student to write responses to the statement. Because the intention is to elicit quick responses, it is useful for the educator to tell students they are not required to think deeply about their reactions, only to record their initial thoughts. Allow three to four minutes for this phase.

Once students have completed this phase, the educator invites the group to discuss their responses in pairs for five to six minutes. This discussion often reveals students' worst fears. Once concerns have been identified and recognised as commonly held anxieties, students may view them as more manageable.

▲ *Add-ons*

Purpose: To encourage participation and ascertain attitudes.
Group Size: This exercise works particularly well with small groups, of
               10–12 students, but can be also used with larger groups.
Time: 30 minutes for 10–12 students, longer for a larger group.
Resources: None.

Activity 1

The educator makes a verbal statement related to a predetermined topic
or theme. Each student is asked to contribute an *add-on*. There are no set
rules about sentence length or presentation style so this type of activity
can, and often does, meander in any and all directions as each student
adds their contribution.

Example:

Statement: *Good listening skills are essential for practitioners working
               in service areas.*
Student 1:   True.
Student 2:   I think we talk to people the way we'd like them to talk to
               us.
Student 3:   Sometimes listening is more important than talking.
Student 4:   I get mad when I have to listen to rubbish.
Student 5:   Why can't people just do something if it's going to help them,
               it's a waste of time having to explain everything to them.
Student 6:   There's a good book on listening skills in the . . . . .
Student 7:   You need to do it, not read about it.
Student 8:   Listening is about looking and watching, taking in how a
               person's behaving, trying to imagine what it would be like
               to be in their situation.
Student 9:   No one can be in anyone else's shoes.
Student 10: There's a saying, something about not criticising until you've
               walked in their moccasins.
Student 11: What have Indians got to do with us?
Student 12: We'll have to work with people from different cultures.
Student 13: Listening is listening, isn't it?

Activity 2

After sufficient rounds the educator asks what learning, if any, has occurred.
After attending to student responses and taking them into account, the

educator gives a mini-lecture about key listening skills, concluding with a story that demonstrates how easily communication can break down when people do not listen thoughtfully. After a general discussion on listening, students form pairs and retell the educator's story to each other. In the retellings, the listeners must use at least one of the key listening skills mentioned in the mini-lecture, for example minimal encouragers or paraphrasing. After the retellings, the educator leads a general discussion to ascertain what changes occurred to the story.

This activity was adapted from an exercise published on the Internet by Wordweave: http:www/welcome.to/Wordweave

▲   *Jump starts*

Purpose: To help generate story ideas.
Group size: This exercise works equally well with small and large groups.
Time: 40 minutes for 10–12 students, longer for a larger group.
Resources: Sentence beginnings, pens and paper.

Activity 1

The educator reads out six sentence beginnings, then asks students to complete all sentences using endings which involve (real or imagined) professional practice situations.

Examples:

- *She arrived late . . .*
- *They were waiting . . .*
- *He turned pale . . .*
- *The door opened . . .*
- *It was a mess . . .*
- *I had nothing to do . . .*

Each student reads their completed sentences to the large group. If time is short students can form pairs and read them to each other.

Examples:

- *She arrived late* so I'd been waiting outside in the storm for a while.
- *They were waiting* for someone to come along and do all the tasks they hated.

- *He turned pale* when I told him the cost.
- *The door opened* and in walked my new manager.
- *It was a mess* from start to finish.
- *I had nothing to do* for the first three minutes then it was bedlam.

Activity 2

Students choose one of their completed sentences to be the first sentence of a story they tell another student. These stories must involve real or imagined professional practice situations.

▲ *Newspaper stories*

Purpose: To encourage creative storytelling.
Group size: This exercise works equally well with small or large groups.
Time: 30 minutes for 10–12 students, longer for a larger group.
Resources: Enlarged newspaper headlines that relate in some way to professional practice, Blu-Tack, whiteboard and pens or pin-board and pins.

Examples

- Teachers seek bonuses
- Refuge head speaks out
- CYFS (Children and Youth and Family Service) defended
- Police struggle to quell street brawl
- Research buoy still missing
- Prolific novelist left no money in will
- Prosecutors frustrated
- Broker upgrades Telecom to 'buy'
- Silver lining will be apparent in end, financial planner promises
- Software firm sets up in NZ (New Zealand)

(*Otago Daily Times*, 15 January 2001)

Activity

Blu-Tack the enlarged newspaper headings to a whiteboard, or display in some other way. Ask each student to choose a headline and write a 50-word story about it. Collect stories (which are, and remain, anonymous), mix them up, then hand them out. Each student reads another student's story to the large group.

▲ *Postcard stories*

Purpose: To encourage viewing situations from two perspectives.
Group size: 10–12 students are ideal. Large groups can be split into several smaller groups.
Time: Activity 1 – 7 to 8 minutes.
              Activity 2 – 7 to 8 minutes
              Activity 3 – 12 to 15 minutes.
              (This exercise has 3 distinct parts.)
Resources: Card or paper set out to resemble postcards, as shown below. A postbox (a cardboard carton can be used). Pens.

Bethany Whitherfield
Placement Coordinator
School of Tourism
Bannockburn Polytechnic
Western Districts
New Zealand

Stamp

Activity 1

The educator asks students to focus on their most recent work experience or clinical placement and to think about the time they were **most engaged** as a learner. To aid recall, the educator suggests students tell each other what it was that made this time memorable. Allow two to three minutes for this phase. The educator then hands out the postcards and asks students to write to their placement coordinator or supervisor, telling a story in 20 words about how this placement or experience advanced their learning.

Activity 2

The educator asks students to focus on their most recent work experience or clinical placement and to think about the time they were **least engaged** as a learner. To aid recall, the educator suggests they tell another student what it was that made this time least valuable. Allow two to three minutes for this phase. The educator then hands out another set of postcards and asks students to write to their placement coordinator or supervisor telling a story in 20 words about how this placement or experience hindered their learning.

Students place both their anonymous postcards in the postbox which the educator delivers to the coordinator/supervisor. The coordinator/supervisor writes responses, also in 20 words, on the flip side of each card.

Activity 3

In the next session, students retrieve their two cards from the box and, in small groups of three to four, tell each other their postcard stories.

This activity was adapted from a postcard exercise designed by Sally Brown and Phil Race (1997) and a feedback exercise designed by Stephen Brookfield and Stephen Preskill (1999).

▲ *Silent stories*

Purpose: To provide opportunities for visual and silent representations of feelings experienced in work or clinical situations.

Group size: This exercise works equally well with small and large groups.

Time: 90 minutes.

Resources: Whatever props are in the room. Cards with a feeling, such as fear, anger or embarrassment, written on them. Post-it notes. An A3 sheet of paper and a pen for each group.

Activity

The educator acts out a feeling such as apprehension through a silent form of expression such as dance or mime, then asks each group to represent this same feeling silently. Each representation must visually depict a real or imagined work situation. Groups are given ten minutes to come up with a situation and decide how they are going to represent it. Group members must not speak during this preparation time but can use pens and paper.

After representing this emotion, each group is asked to select a card and represent the feeling written on it. One group at a time presents their chosen feeling. Observers must decide what feeling is being portrayed and write it on a Post-it, also noting what they observed that caused them to come to their decision. These post-its are given to the group after the performance and time is provided so feedback can be taken into account before moving to the final phase.

In the final phase of this activity, each group is assigned another (different) feeling and asked to tell a visual but silent story about it. Each story must be set in an imagined or real work setting and include inanimate objects (using whatever is in the room and in the students' possession) and authentic characters. No spoken communication is allowed. Emphasis is on silent representation of emotions in stories and the silent interpretations of them.

Using Post-its with the following sentence starters written on them, observers record their impressions of each performing group.

- I think the feeling being portrayed was . . . .
- I think the objects were . . .
- I think the roles played included . . .
- I think the scene was about . . .

These Post-its are presented to each group after its performance is complete. The educator asks each group of students to consider the feedback silently, then on an A3 sheet of paper, write their account of their performance on the top third of the paper. In the middle section they write their observers' accounts, using the information on the Post-it sentence starters. On the third section they note any differences between the two accounts. Each sheet is pinned or Blu-Tacked on a wall. The educator requests that students move around the room and read each group's sheet, reflecting silently on their learning.

▲ *I remember . . .*

Purpose: To highlight the challenges inherent in everyday professional practice.
Group size: This exercise works equally well with small and large groups.
Time: 60 minutes.
Resources: Pens and paper.

Activity 1

The educator asks students to think of an unsatisfactory interaction they had recently with a professional person, perhaps a physiotherapist, an accountant, a lawyer, a doctor or a dentist. Using this memory, the student begins a story with the words 'I remember'.

Example
> I remember when I went to see a doctor because I was feeling really tired. I had a sore throat and my glands were up. She'd arranged for

me to have some tests for the same thing a few months ago. When I went to get the results she said she wasn't sure what the tests meant. She said she didn't do them very often because they were so hard to read. Hearing that didn't give me much confidence or make me feel any better and I got the feeling she was distracted. She was typing notes on to the computer, asking me about my exams and what I was doing over the holidays and flicking through a text she had on her desk, all at the same time. Because I'd been feeling unwell for ages I said I wanted to see a specialist. She told me who to contact and said she'd send a letter later that day. I couldn't get into the specialist for six weeks and when I did see him, he hadn't received a letter from my doctor. I was so mad and felt really embarrassed. I changed my doctor the following week.

Activity 2

Once students have written their 'I remember' stories, the educator asks them to write another story, using the first person, about the same situation but from the professionals' perspective. The intention is to consider what may have been happening for that professional on that particular day.

Example

What a day! Every child in town has the 'flu and I've seen a third of them. My own two have it as well. My usual caregiver couldn't look after them so I had to ring around. Eventually my sister came but she wasn't happy, she's got her own problems but she needs the money so said yes. Why do these things always happen when James [partner] is out of town? By the time I arrived at work, the waiting room was over-flowing. I checked my appointments and was so mad when I saw that the receptionist had scheduled me extra patients. I'd promised to get home early. I made a note to phone my sister, grabbed a cup of coffee and started work. The first three patients had detailed lists of aches and pains and they wanted to talk about them all so I was behind schedule by 9.30am. By late afternoon, I'd seen numerous infected throats and ears. One child really worried me. After she left I checked a text because I was half wondering if there was something more serious going on. I was still flicking through it when my next patient came in. Like me she's a busy professional. I really like talking to her but didn't have time today. I did remember to ask her about her exams though because I remember she'd said on an earlier visit that she was anxious about them. She presented with similar symptoms to her last visit. I'd done some tests but hadn't checked the results. I checked them while she was there, pretty inconclusive but I agreed when she asked to see a specialist. I was really pushed for time so made a note to write the referral letter then walked out with her and called my next patient. The day just got worse and I was still worried about the child who had presented with flu symptoms but might have something more serious. By the time I got home to my sister and two distressed children I was exhausted.

Activity 3

The educator asks for volunteers to read their dual perspective stories to the group. After several dual stories have been read, the educator leads a discussion on the realities of everyday practice. What are the challenges? Why do things get out of hand? How can things be managed to meet both the professional's needs and their client's/patient's needs?

▲ *Arbitrary story structures*

Purpose: To encourage creative storytelling using arbitrary structures.
Group size: This exercise works equally well with small and large groups.
Time: 40 minutes per story structure activity.
Resources: Instructions, story structures, whiteboard and pens or an overhead projector and transparency, pens and paper.

The following instructions are written on a whiteboard or transparency.

1.   Choose one story structure.
2.   Read Part 1 of the arbitrary story structure and write the first paragraph of your story.
3.   Read Part 2 and write the second paragraph.
4.   Continue the process, writing a paragraph for each part.
5.   Read your story silently or aloud.
6.   If you think it is worth developing further, make notes about how you could do this, then put your notes aside until you are ready to develop them in some way, perhaps as a short story, article or poem.

Arbitrary story structure 1: The journey

Part 1:   You are on your way somewhere.
Part 2:   You see something that has an impact on you.
Part 3:   You think about what you have seen.
Part 4:   You experience a strong emotion.
Part 5:   You meet someone you know.

Part 6:   You tell them about what you saw.
Part 7:   You decide on your profession.

Arbitrary story structure 2: Eavesdropping

Part 1:   You are at work.
Part 2:   You overhear a conversation.
Part 3:   You think about what you heard.
Part 4:   You make a change.

Arbitrary story structure 3: The question

Part 1:   You are new to the workplace.
Part 2:   Someone approaches and speaks to you.
Part 3:   You answer and a conversation takes place.
Part 4:   You walk away thinking about the person you had the conversation with.
Part 5:   You remember something about the conversation.
Part 6:   You see something in your surroundings that answers a question you thought of during the conversation.

This activity has been adapted from The Writer's Path: A Guidebook for your Creative Journey, *Todd Walton and Mindy Toomay, 2000.*

▲ *Abstract story structures*

Purpose: To begin stories from evocative word starters.
Group size: This exercise works equally well with small and large groups.
Time: 40 minutes per story structure activity.
Resources: Instructions, story structures, whiteboard and pens or an overhead projector and transparency, pens and paper.

The following instructions are written on a whiteboard or overhead transparency.

1.   Choose a story structure.
2.   Read the first part of the structure. Take a moment for the word to evoke an image or thought, then write the first paragraph of your story.
3.   Continue this process for subsequent parts of the structure until you have written a paragraph for each.
4.   Read your story silently or aloud.
5.   If you think it is worth developing further, make notes about how you could do this, then put your notes aside until you are ready to develop them in some way.

Abstract story structure 1

Part 1:　Home
Part 2:　Message
Part 3:　Car
Part 4:　Meeting
Part 5:　Frustration
Part 6:　Conversation
Part 7:　Solution

Abstract story structure 2

Part 1:　Laughter
Part 2:　Walking
Part 3:　Package
Part 4:　Remembering
Part 5:　Rain
Part 6:　Desk
Part 7:　Phone

Abstract story structure 3

Part 1:　Glimpse
Part 2:　Music
Part 3:　Person
Part 4:　Conversation
Part 5:　Joy
Part 6:　Beginning

This activity has been adapted from The Writer's Path: A Guidebook for your Creative Journey, *Todd Walton and Mindy Toomay, 2000.*

▲　*Diamond nine*

Purpose:　　To identify key elements within stories.
Group size:　This exercise works equally well with small and large groups.
Time:　　　45 minutes.
Resources:　Post-its and pens.

The educator asks students to think of a story they have told about their practice in the last week and to write nine different things about it, one on each of nine Post-its. After completing this task, the educator instructs students to arrange their Post-its in a diamond shape with the most important aspect of the story at the top and the least important in ninth position.

```
        1
     2   3
   4   5   6
     7   8
        9
```

The educator asks students to reflect on their prioritising, giving particular consideration to Post-it 1. What is written on it? Is it a feeling, a place, a person or an action? What might the order of storytelling elements signify? Does the ninth aspect in some way represent what is resolved/unresolved? After students have taken time to consider these questions, the educator asks them to form pairs. Taking a Post-it which has an element on it that they are happy to share, each partner tells the other a three-minute story about it. In this activity, students have control over which elements they share and which stories they tell.

This activity was adapted from a diamond nine exercise designed by Sally Brown and Phil Race, 1997.

▲ Re-framing experience stories

Purpose: To re-imagine and retell stories.
Group size: This exercise works equally well with small and large groups.
Time: 60 minutes.
Resources: Post-its and pens.

The educator asks students to take nine Post-its, number them (1–9) and write the following headings.

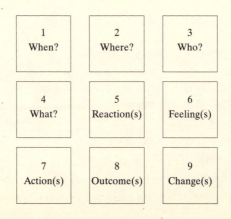

1 When?	2 Where?	3 Who?
4 What?	5 Reaction(s)	6 Feeling(s)
7 Action(s)	8 Outcome(s)	9 Change(s)

The educator then asks students to think of a practice situation or event that caused you to question their beliefs or assumptions, then write responses to the following questions (response 1 on Post-it 1, response 2 on Post-it 2 and so on):

1. When did it happen?
2. Where did it happen?
3. Who (write roles only, not names) was involved?
4. What happened?
5. How did you react?
6. How did you feel?
7. Who (role not name) attempted to take control of the situation?
8. How successful were they?
9. If you could change the way you managed the situation, what would you do?

The educator asks students to read through their notes and to re-frame their stories by incorporating the change(s) they identified on Post-it 9, then to form pairs and tell their re-imagined story (in first person) to their partner. Students are asked by the educator to end their re-framed stories by completing the following line: 'Telling my story this way has made me feel . . .'.

▲ *Post-it parade*

Purpose: To identify storylines (themes) within stories.
Group size: This exercise works equally well with small and large groups.
Time: 25 minutes.
Resources: Post-its and pens.

Activity

The educator presents students with a series of tasks.

1. Think of a practice-related situation that is currently intriguing you.
2. If you were to tell a story about this 'situation', what would the storyline or theme be?
3. Write this storyline on a Post-it.
4. Share your storyline in pairs.
5. Use reflective questioning to explore why each of you chose your particular situation.

6.   Identify possible implications for self and practice if you were to explore, and reflect on, this situation in more depth.
7.   If this exercise raised issues that remain unresolved, tell your partner how you will care for yourself and describe what action(s) you will take to move towards resolution.

▲ *Workplace of dreams*

Purpose: To identify professional aspirations and values.
Group size: This exercise works equally well with small and large groups.
Time: 45 minutes.
Resources: Paper and pens.

Activity 1

Educator says the following:

'Close your eyes and relax. Allow yourself to enter the workplace of your dreams. What images come to mind? What does your workplace look like, smell like? Who is there? How do they greet you? What is your position? What is your first task?'

The educator then presents a series of tasks.

1.   Take a few minutes to write a descriptive paragraph about your dream workplace.
2.   In pairs, read your stories aloud.
3.   Now tell your story to another person as though you are actually living it, for example:

> I'm walking up the stairs. I hear laughter. I push open the door and walk up to reception. I smell flowers. The chairs look comfortable and there are a couple of couches, big squashy ones, I feel at home. Next thing I'm surrounded by people, all ages, all sizes. They're expecting me. Six, maybe seven, people welcome me. By the time they've introduced themselves I feel like an old friend. I smell real coffee. Someone shows me my office. It's well equipped, overlooks the park and should get early morning sun. I touch the desk, make it mine, then follow everyone into an open area. There's an enormous table. Everyone's sitting around drinking coffee and laughing. What looks like a script is written on a whiteboard. Looks exciting, challenging. I can't wait to be involved. 'Take a pew,' Laura says. Geoff hands me

coffee. 'Welcome to the team,' says Mike, 'pitch in with some ideas when you feel ready.'

Activity 2

After stories have been shared, the educator asks students to read their stories silently and circle key words or phrases. Then, in pairs, students identify what aspirations and values are apparent in their circled key words or phases and say how they envisage incorporating them into their practice.

▲ *What if?*

Purpose: To encourage group storytelling.
Group size: This exercise works equally well with small and large groups.
Time: 40 minutes.
Resources: A set of scenarios.

Activity
Educator presents a different 'what if' scenario to each group.

Example 1
What if you find yourself alone in a room at your workplace and a person, obviously upset and possibly confused, comes through the door asking for assistance?

Example 2
What if you are asked to perform a task that you do not feel ready to undertake?

Example 3
What if you find yourself in a situation where you think you have a solution to a problem but you are the least senior person present?

The educator asks students to come up with a group story that they can tell to the large group to demonstrate how they would handle their imagined scenario. Working with stories in this way alerts students to the complex and diverse situations they may encounter in everyday practice.

This activity was triggered after reading Anne Bernays and Pamela Painter's What If? Writing Exercises for Fiction Writers, 1990.

▲ *No, that's not what happened*

Purpose: To shift stories in creative and spontaneous ways.
Group size: This exercise works equally well with small and large groups as long as there are an even number of students.
Time: 5–6 minutes for demonstration, 10–15 minutes for each subsequent story.
Resources: None.

The educator and a volunteer from the group demonstrate how a 'No, that's not what happened' story is told. Then, in pairs, each student takes turns at being teller of a story and interjector in their partner's story. The teller's role is to begin telling a story about a situation they were involved in or observed. The interjector's role is to say from time to time (not too frequently), 'No, that's not what happened' to which the teller must answer some version of 'You're right, that's not what happened, what really happened was,' and take the story down a different track.

Example

Teller: It was a stressful time for me, nearly the end of the year. I was studying part time, bringing up a family and working full time. I was driving home from work, thinking 'What am I going to make for dinner?' I was wondering if I should stop for pizza when I noticed an elderly man on the footpath looking like he wanted to use the pedestrian crossing. I slowed down, then stopped. I was still thinking about dinner when I realised the passenger door had opened and the man was getting into the front seat.

Interjector: No, that's not what happened.

Teller: You're right, he didn't get into the front seat, he got into the back. I stopped thinking about dinner and checked the rear vision mirror to see how many cars were behind me. Heaps, and one driver was tooting so I started driving. I couldn't believe this stranger was sitting in my car. I looked in the mirror again, took a good look at him. He had a big coat on, the collar was right up under his chin. I started to imagine what he might have under his coat then I remembered what my friend who works in mental health told me when I went overseas for the first time. She said, 'If you find yourself in a tricky situation, make yourself human'. So I started talking about everything, my kids, my dog, my dad. I said he'd fought in the war, then I talked about gardening . . .

Interjector: No, that's not what happened.

Teller: No, you're right, I talked about camping before gardening. Then I drove up on the curb and bounced the car down so hard that the old chaps' hands popped out of his pockets. That's right, before that he had both hands in his coat pockets. You can imagine what I thought. When I turned to check if he was okay, he was twiddling with a button and making some strange muttering noise. I wondered if I should go to the police station, drive right up the steps and through the glass doors.

Interjector: No, that's not what happened.

Teller: You're right, I didn't do it but I thought about it. Then he started reciting what sounded like the names of vegetables. I told him I didn't know there were so many. He laughed this strange laugh just as I had to stop for the lights, so I had a chance to turn around and look at him again. He had no teeth and the skin under his eyes hung down in folds, I counted four before I noticed his glass eye.

Interjector: No, that's not what happened.

Teller: You're right, he didn't have a glass eye but his eye was an unusual colour and reminded me of an uncle's eye which was made from glass. He lost it when his brother shot him in the head with an arrow made from our willow tree.

Interjector: No, that's not what happened.

Teller: You're right. He lost it when an intruder broke into his house and attacked him with a poker. That's what might've happened to me if I hadn't kept my wits. The old chap kept trying to say something. He was getting mad so I did what I should have done in the first place – I slammed on the brakes, turned around to face him and said, 'Get out of my car this instant'. That's when he pulled his teeth out of his pocket, put them in his mouth and said, 'I was trying to tell you to stop. I live here'. He pointed to Resthaven, a home for the elderly. 'Now how much do I owe?' He thought I was a taxi. I felt such a fool but it could've been dangerous, couldn't it?

This activity was first encountered when Angie Farrow used it during a Creative Planning workshop at the University of Victoria, Wellington, New Zealand, 2000.

▲ *Structured storytelling*

Purpose: To encourage creative connections between stories.
Group size: This exercise works equally well with small and large groups.
Time: 90 minutes.
Resources: Paper and pens.

The educator guides students through several stages, each of which involves a different task. Some students may wish to make notes during some of the stages.

Task 1 (Individual)
Think of a journey you have taken.
Where did you depart from?
Where did you arrive?

Task 2 (In pairs)
Interview each other to extract details. Allow 10 minutes for each person. The purpose is to reveal:

a)   Exterior physical world, e.g. landscape, weather.
b)   Personal relationships, e.g. teller's world from social perspective.
c)   Internal world, e.g. feelings, beliefs, values.

Establish when you departed:
Who were you with?
What did you take?
How did you feel?
What was around you?
What was the weather like?

Establish when you arrived:
What did the place look and smell like?
How did you feel about arriving?
What was your most memorable moment of the journey?
What was your most powerful physical image?

Task 3 (Groups of 4)

Each student relates to the group the story they heard (not told) while in pairs. The teller draws on details revealed during the interview and relates the story in first person. At the end of the story the group may ask questions. The teller must make up what they do not know. Allow 4 minutes for each story, 16 minutes in total.

Task 4 (Individual)

Choose one of the stories you heard in your group (not your own), work it into shape (written note form) so you can tell it conversationally. Then add one new element from one of the other stories you heard in your group (can be something from your own).

Task 5 (Educator)

The educator asks three or four students to tell their stories. The educator may want to try and identify the student (from the group) who went on the initial, real or imagined journey in each of the stories.

This activity was first encountered when Simon O'Connor used it at a Creative Writing Summer School in Dunedin, New Zealand, 1999.

CHARTING DISTANCES

The storytelling activities we have outlined offer educators and students opportunities to imagine experiences creatively or recall others that in some way depict aspects of professional life. The distance between imagining what it is like to be a professional and actively participating on a daily basis in a professional capacity is immense. If students do not consider situations they may encounter in practice then the distance between 'creatively imagining' and 'actively participating' remains uncharted until students are fully employed in their professional roles. Reflective strategies such as storytelling and creative writing activities have significant roles to play in preparing students to chart these distances. Different activities highlight different aspects of practice and although we have offered a range, readers may wish to design their own activities.

DESIGNING STORYTELLING ACTIVITIES

Designing activities that encourage students to use, enjoy and learn from storytelling takes time, energy and thoughtful consideration. Like other learning tools, storytelling can be both over and under-used. It is imperative, therefore, that educators carefully consider which activities to use with which group of students for which purpose. We suggest educators use the activities and processes we have outlined in this text, and those which they design themselves, personally before introducing them to students.

Our approach, to help determine whether storytelling is the most suitable learning tool to teach a particular topic or aspect of the curriculum, has been to ask ourselves ten questions:

1. Is storytelling the most compelling and memorable way for this group of students to learn about this topic and if so, why?
2. What outcomes do we want this group of students to achieve?
3. Will these outcomes be assessed, and if so, how?
4. Which type of storytelling activity best suits these students' learning needs?
5. How will we ensure against inappropriate levels of disclosure?
6. What forms of support are required for students and educators involved in the activity?
7. How long will this storytelling activity take to design, trial and implement?
8. Who will be involved in the design, trial and feedback phases?
9. When will this activity be ready to use with students?
10. How will this activity be evaluated?

Only after we have answered these questions to our satisfaction do we begin working on a new activity or process. We have found that if we follow a few simple guidelines and avoid the pitfalls, our activities largely meet our teaching purposes and the students' learning needs. We offer our guidelines in the form of tips and traps.

Tips

• Do trial new activities with colleagues before using them with students.
• Do keep instructions simple.
• Do have a specific purpose for each activity and articulate what that purpose is to students.
• Do allow enough time for each activity to be fully realised.

- Do consider ethical issues.
- Do provide access to forms of support if the activity is likely to raise significant emotional reactions.
- Do consider whether formal or informal assessment is best suited to the activity.
- Do cater for all learning styles by introducing a range of oral, written, physical and visual storytelling activities.
- Do take cultural storytelling differences into account.
- Do encourage creative interpretations of activities.
- Do elicit feelings in safe and manageable ways.
- Do encourage active participation.
- Do ensure confidentiality issues are addressed.
- Do have fun.

Traps

- Don't introduce demanding storytelling activities before students have experienced and gained confidence with a range of oral, written, silent, visual and physical forms.
- Don't expect everyone to feel comfortable with every activity.
- Don't be afraid of silence. Some stories take time.
- Don't persevere with a storytelling activity if it is not working. Some activities will appeal to some groups and not to others.
- Don't over-assess.
- Don't set students up to reveal more than they might feel comfortable with.
- Don't over-use storytelling. Like any learning tool, it can become mundane.
- Don't hijack student stories with response stories.
- Don't forget about the unspoken stories – they reveal themselves in many ways.

Whether educators use or modify existing activities and processes or design their own, storytelling is a learning tool with considerable potential. Students from a multitude of disciplines, studying at a range of levels, can learn about themselves and their professions through storytelling. How students manage the *story finding* stage varies between individuals. However, educators who purposefully and thoughtfully create a storytelling culture within their classrooms provide a foundation for the following stages. In Chapter 6 we focus on *story telling* within professional practice settings.

6 Telling Stories about Practice

Learning to work in practice settings is a difficult and often challenging aspect of becoming professional. While there are many demands and uncertainties for students, it is possible for them to become more comfortable with professional environments through stories. For many students, such familiarity occurs by listening to stories told by other professionals. Through these stories knowledge is shared, hints are given about skill application, and attitudes inherent in professional settings are made overt. Stories also provide students with opportunities to notice and connect with contexts or environments and, through listening to stories, begin to make sense of practice realities and the relationships between current and past experience. In particular, there are unique learning opportunities for students when they engage in *storytelling*, the second stage in our model.

STORYTELLING

Gradually, as students are provided with opportunities to engage more fully in professional work environments, they too have stories to share. It is important for educators to encourage students to work with their stories soon after their initial contact with professional settings. Even though these early stories may seem insignificant to the students, and lack the drama of those shared by more experienced practitioners, it is important to explore and examine the students' practice realities to enable further learning to occur. While it is usual for students to feel some hesitancy, because such sharing could reveal a lack of competence and confidence, it provides a way in which day-to-day issues can be resolved, possible alternative approaches discussed and relevant theory applied.

To move to a place where stories are valued and recognised as integral to the construction of knowledge and related to development of practice, it is necessary to engage students in storytelling processes that assist them to understand practice events and enable layers of meaning to be uncovered. This approach utilises connections with context and past experience, enabling students to make meaning of their current practice by clarifying aspects of their stories. The processes outlined in this chapter provide guidelines for activities that are suitable for use with undergraduate students engaged in the beginning stage of professional education.

LEARNING THROUGH LISTENING

Being placed in a professional setting, such as a new ward or classroom, can be daunting. While students often comment on the difficulty of being in unfamiliar surroundings and not knowing what will happen at given times, their underlying concern frequently relates to their feelings of general unease and uncertainty about being able to cope. This unease can involve such a level of anxiety about performing particular tasks, such as writing legibly on a whiteboard, completing specific assessments or giving an injection, that it is difficult for students also to incorporate more general observations of the contexts in which they practice. The cause of anxiety may stem from a more nebulous reality, with an underlying questioning of ability to deal with complex situations in appropriate ways. Such generalised anxiety is likely to impact negatively on students' ability to undertake, appropriately complete or document tasks that can be successfully demonstrated in situations that are perceived as less stressful.

Listening to stories that reveal how experienced practitioners work with complex situations can provide insights into practice realities as appropriate responses are shared and the skills needed are identified. Stories also illustrate which attitudes and values are considered important in particular contexts. In fact, when listening to stories about practice events, it is helpful to encourage students to consider which attitudes and values are present, as these can expose the meaning of experiences.

Stories shaping meaning

The degree to which a person who is entering a new environment develops a shared meaning of events with those already working there is called 'intersubjectivity' (Adams, 1994; Tharp and Gallimore, 1988). This is more than just understanding terminology, instructions or a story that is told. It is a process whereby it is possible to appreciate the reasons for actions and value similar professional outcomes. Within this process it is usual for newcomers gradually to incorporate into their vocabulary new words and, in particular, abbreviations for actions or events. Initially, such language signifies a sense of belonging to a professional group. Gradually it becomes the means through which complex procedures or realities can be easily expressed and precise meanings shared.

Much learning that occurs when students are initially exposed to practice realities involves building templates by which common practice occurrences are managed (Smagorinsky, 1995). For example, a shorthand term such as 'doing obs' in the nursing world involves performing a series of 'observa- tions' related to a particular patient. These observations include a number of activities, such as taking a patient's temperature, monitoring blood pres- sure, pulse and respiration rate, and will also involve general observations of the colour, level of comfort and consciousness of the patient. In specific settings there might be additional procedures that are incorporated into such a template due to specific health problems. Similarly, beginning teachers discover that 'preparing a lesson' requires familiarity with a partic- ular curriculum subject, focusing on specific desired outcomes, gathering relevant resources and choosing appropriate learning activities and assessment processes, while being aware of the specific learning needs and difficulties of a particular group of students.

While tasks included in these activities are learned individually within a formal environment then placed in relationship to each other, the importance, value and centrality of each to professional practice is fre- quently only learned through stories. Comments such as 'When I was taking the obs/or preparing a lesson, I noticed . . .' or 'I was going down to take Mr Smiths obs/prepare a Year 4 lesson, when all of a sudden . . .', place these activities within the day-to-day practice reality of more experienced colleagues. This type of comment then enables individuals to be confirmed as having a place in professional practice rather than simply being involved in related skills.

The complexity and quantity of practice-related terms and new ideas could be overwhelming for students. Rather than being excited and challenged to incorporate language and ideas such as formative and summative assessment, IEPs (Individualised Education Programmes) or health promotion into their vocabulary, students may experience frustration and confusion. Stories can assist them by placing terminology within a known and understood practice experience or framework so that complex jargon is demystified. Through this process it is important to hold the complexity of the concept intact but provide sufficient support or scaffolding to enable meaning-making to occur (Smith, 1988; Vygotsky, 1978).

In addition to learning about language and templates, stories can enable identification of what is important. While academically there are opportunities to discover the relationships between theory and practice, becoming attuned to stories and developing intersubjectivity enables students to identify affective components. These components are central to stories and can significantly influence students' perceptions, thus shaping their understanding of events (Tharp and Gallimore, 1988). Sharing stories for the purpose of cathartic release is particularly powerful because significant levels of affective information are revealed. Likewise, when educators use humorous or dramatic stories to place new theoretical concepts into a practice reality, it is possible to make the learning more relevant and place the information more carefully in relation to the students' existing knowledge.

Listeners shaping stories

Finding the meaning of messages within stories is not just the responsibility of tellers. By their very nature oral stories also involve listeners. The type of relationship between tellers and listeners, and their connectedness with experience, has a significant impact on their ability to make sense and then meaning through stories. Listeners to a particular story may not always interpret events in the same way as the teller or other listeners. Past experience, the degree of shared meaning or intersubjectivity, and current values will impact on what is understood in a particular situation. Therefore, a group supposedly sharing a similar learning situation, such as teachers learning about classroom management, or nurses learning to do a dressing will, because of their varied life experiences and personal values, place different interpretations on the learning experience (Manning and Payne, 1993). This is particularly likely to occur if stories are used to reinforce key points or illustrate application of theory, because the underlying message of stories can frequently be quite subtle.

Stories from practice also facilitate learning but will be interpreted by students in relation to their self-perception, level of confidence, or attitudes and values about what is important. A story may be heard by one listener in its entirety with an assumption that the underlying attitudes and values form an essential part of a particular action, while another listener may question aspects of the story or propose alternative approaches. Rarely is this an either/or situation because awareness of alternative options is usually at a conscious level while assumptions about, and acceptance of, underlying attitudes and values are frequently at the subconscious level.

Reactions can also vary from one situation to another depending on the confidence levels of students in a given situation and their knowledge of related theoretical underpinnings. If a story moves beyond a listener's level of competence, the primary focus is likely to remain with the affective components rather than the underlying theory as related to practice. Therefore, the degree to which shared meaning is developed becomes an essential element if there is an expectation that particular outcomes will be achieved (Tudge, 1991).

When there is emphasis on application of knowledge to practice, as frequently occurs in professions such as nursing, teaching and occupational therapy, stories about practice realities are particularly important. Practitioners who are actively engaged in professional practice provide a level of face validity or authenticity through their stories, which may not be perceived in strictly theoretical presentations. Many educators attempt to readdress this problem, and establish credibility as practitioners, by sharing their own experiences as part of their teaching. While this strategy is usually very effective, it is important to incorporate the process of dealing with day-to-day realities, along with dramatic situations, to ensure students appreciate and value the whole spectrum of practice realities. Failure to incorporate such aspects can result in students placing less value on ordinary events, and, as a result, they may lack interest in gaining competence in these settings. On the other hand, failure to use stories in teaching situations can result in students having difficulty applying theory to practice.

Listening to stories enables those new to practice settings to gain entry into the shared world of events and experiences that make up their professions. As experience is gained, it is important for students to find their own voice and tell their own stories. When students work with their stories they can enter into dialogue about what they have experienced, be involved in critique of practice, receive affirmation and engage in ongoing learning.

LEARNING THROUGH TELLING

Stories shared within practice contexts are usually spontaneous and informal, so result primarily in catharsis. They arise from a need to share embarrassing, sad, confusing or joyous moments with others. While it is important to acknowledge the value of cathartic release, response to such stories frequently involves listeners sharing their own experiences through *response stories.* This can be frustrating for tellers who have specific questions they want discussed or information they need clarified. To encourage dialogue, tellers may end their stories with specific questions, however, in informal settings, these may not be addressed. Tellers who are dissatisfied may need to seek other opportunities to address their concerns.

If learning is to occur from experience, it is necessary for students to engage in the additional process of reflective dialogue. From such dialogue it is possible to facilitate the integration of practice and theory and enable practice realities to be seen as a basis for assignments required for academic purposes. In educational settings, exemplars can be written to illustrate particular issues or demonstrate comprehension of certain processes. Such assignments can be used to encourage students to find their personal storytelling voice in ways that can advance practice. Rather than attempting to move straight into written stories, we find it useful to begin by encouraging students to tell stories about practice experiences.

Telling stories

Storytelling is most commonly part of an oral tradition, and therefore it is appropriate to begin the process by asking students to share a story with one or two peers. Educators need to make storytellers aware that when they choose stories, they may be shared later with a larger student group as part of a general discussion or to provide an illustration about some aspect of practice. Thus, what begins as primarily a small group discussion may extend to a wider audience.

It is rarely useful to process stories if tellers are not keyplayers. Other people may have told tellers stories or events may have been observed. If tellers and listeners attempt to work with these stories they frequently find that they have insufficient knowledge about the key players' motivations and past experience, or about the wider contexts, to enable adequate processing. It is therefore unlikely that appropriate and effective outcomes can result, and frequently negative and judgemental projection occurs. Even if these stories are viewed as positive, without the key players' perspectives, they are of limited value because important aspects remain unknown. However, such stories can be explored if tellers identify their roles in relation to them.

A new lecturer shared this story.

> I was on my way to the staffroom to deliver a message. As I passed a colleague's room I looked through the window and saw her standing

over a student yelling at him. I know she didn't see me. I was horrified but I didn't know what to do, so I did nothing.

Likewise, if tellers wish to recount stories they heard from other people, processing is more successful if it is framed with the current teller identifying a key role as demonstrated in the following story.

I was having coffee with a friend who told me that the Registered Nurse she was on night shift with told her not to bother checking patients regularly during the night – she said 'if they want something they'll ring.' My friend was a bit concerned at first but said that it made her duties easier. I was worried but did not know what to say.

Once such stories have been reframed in these ways, it is possible to process them more successfully.

EXPANDING STORIES

Storytelling opportunities at this stage are primarily to encourage tellers and listeners to begin reflecting on practice. Tellers usually outline the main aspects of their stories, but frequently there are other aspects that can be expanded so listeners are encouraged to ask questions and seek clarification. Where and when did it happen? How did the teller feel and how did others react? Why does the teller think the event happened this way or why did others react as they did?

The purpose of these discussions is to expand stories, facilitate articulation of feelings and to enable tellers to engage in some form of reflection. This is not the time for listeners to offer similar stories or share their ideas about how it could have been different. Focus is on examination of the teller's story, enabling it to be developed and understood as fully as possible.

Initially, it may be sufficient to suggest a couple of minutes per teller for a story to be shared with a small group, but as tellers become more experienced in creating helpful dialogue it is useful to allow at least five to ten minutes per teller. With experience, both tellers and listeners become more competent in sharing details of events and it becomes easier for them to engage in dialogue based on stories.

Tellers and listeners need to have multiple opportunities to share their stories and it is advantageous to change group membership for each storytelling session. Dialogue will be shaped in different ways in various clusters and, as listeners hear others engage in useful discussion, they learn how to model their own responses to stories. With a wider range of questions being asked by listeners to prompt tellers to discuss their experiences, it is also more likely that tellers will gain insights into their practice. Through this collaborative process (Jonassen *et al.,* 1995) students learn from each other and demonstrate mutual support that is consistent with working in the bi-directional zone of proximal development (Tudge, 1990). Such dialogue helps move tellers and listeners towards a reflective approach to their practice, although they will continue to experience some cathartic release. When students are comfortable with oral storytelling and the associated dialogue, it is appropriate to make the transition to written storytelling.

Writing stories

The move from oral to written stories can be accomplished by adding another stage to the oral storytelling group process. After each student in the group has told their story and engaged in dialogue to explore and expand understanding of their event, it is helpful if educators then ask tellers to write about their stories. Dialogue, which has been part of the oral telling, assists students to incorporate more detail into their story, and, more importantly, to choose what focus they wish to emphasise during this written phase.

This process requires time and it is important that there is a quiet, undemanding atmosphere. Creating such an atmosphere introduces students to more formal storytelling settings. If students have questions that arise while they are writing, they are usually more appropriately dealt with on a one-to-one basis with the educator moving to the student with the query so that loud talk does not distract other students in the group. It is important that this process is not rushed. It will usually take 15–20 minutes. As students become more competent at identifying details and adding their thoughts, reactions and feelings about their stories, it may be more appropriate to allow 20–25 minutes.

In this *story expanding* stage, students are actively engaged in making meaning (Moon, 1999). Initially, working with insights gained from peer discussion is sufficient. However, as the students' confidence grows, it is useful to incorporate some structures that provide additional ways in which they can focus on their stories to gain insights.

Exploring stories

At this stage of working with written stories, it is helpful to provide a relatively straightforward process that enables further understanding of the various dimensions of the practice event. Once this is accomplished it is possible to work with stories in ways that uncover further layers of meaning. There are a number of ways in which stories can be explored and developed. Initially, it is helpful to focus the process around particular aspects such as identification and examination of key players or tellers' feelings.

Identifying the roles of key players can assist students to appreciate the bigger picture, of which this event is but a part. While initially it is usual for students to focus on those actually present at an event, with thought, the key players are often extended to include others such as family, administrative staff or even politicians! In contrast, identification of feelings provides students with insight into the positive and negative affective responses they experienced during the event (Boud, Keogh and Walker, 1985).

When first embarking on this, the aspect which is the focus of the analysis of the story – key players or feelings – needs to be clearly identified, otherwise the process becomes overwhelming. In time, and with experience, combinations of key players and feelings inevitably merge as inter-relationship and interdependence becomes evident.

It is helpful to use a specific structure such as a template when working formally with stories as this assists students to undertake thorough, in-depth exploration of events and also enables the process to be guided. To aid this stage we have developed a five-stage process:

- naming the primary focus and identifying key responses;
- identifying other responses;
- linking with significant events;
- debriefing in small groups;
- creating a title.

To clarify the process, each of these stages is now discussed in more detail, with emphasis on how feelings might be explored.

- **Naming the primary focus and identifying key responses**. The initial stage is to identify whether the focus is going to relate to feelings or roles of key players. When focusing on feelings, as in this example, the process begins by identifying any key feeling(s) the teller was aware of at the end of the event, and after sharing the story. These are recorded in the second column under 'Key responses'. Usually there is one key feeling; however, sometimes two or even three may be identified.

- **Identifying other responses**. It is then helpful to explore the range of feelings that were evident as the story unfolded. These are recorded in the second column alongside the relevant section of the story script. At this stage there is often clarification of the story and a desire to rework part of the script so that it more accurately reflects the teller's intent. This is a working document and thus accommodates such modifications. The use of double spacing on the template is helpful as it allows for such additions and alterations. Tellers work through their stories to identify changes in intensity or type of feeling. Frequently there are a number of feelings involved, some of which may seem in opposition to each other, such as optimism followed later by frustration.

- **Linking with significant events**. In this stage the teller examines the script of the story as it relates to the feelings that have been identified. A phrase or brief statement is used to explain, clarify or illustrate each feeling that has been named and this is placed in the 'significant events' column. Sometimes there are a number of smaller issues that lead to a change. Capturing this complexity can be particularly helpful in gaining an understanding of the interrelation between various aspects. This part of the process frequently takes considerable time and often is not completed until the tellers have an opportunity to clarify their thinking in small groups. Therefore it is useful to allow a specific amount of time for writing – say 15–20 minutes – and encourage ongoing work through the next stage.

- **Debriefing in small groups**. With some insights into their story, it is useful to provide tellers with an opportunity to share these with one or two peers. Rather than reworking the whole of the story, this is a chance to identify specific aspects of their work in which they have developed an interest, or areas where they wish to seek further clarification. This process enables tellers to refine their thinking within the small group and also to develop new ideas though the responses or questions that come from listeners.

- **Creating a title**. While a working title for the story may arise at various stages along the process, it is useful to return to this aspect and give it further consideration. Once the processing is complete, tellers are asked to provide the title for their story. This 'naming' is held back until after the reflective processes as it gives tellers an opportunity to place their event in a broader context and to identify learning that has occurred. The title can reflect the actual event, the feelings, or the outcome.

When the focus is on key players, tellers identify those they consider fill this role in their story. It is interesting to ponder over who has been excluded. It may be a student who is the focus of a meeting between teachers and psychologists, a patient who is unconscious, or someone who is not initially perceived as playing an important role in the event. It is then useful to identify other individuals the event directly impacts on. While family can be quite evident, others, such as close friends, may be overlooked. Likewise managers, supervisors or coordinators, whose dictates may directly impact on the event, may not initially be seen as important in terms of outcome.

Once tellers have had experience with each of these areas of focus, they may spontaneously combine the various elements. This is a very positive move as it helps reveal the complexity of situations and such processes should be encouraged. In addition, as competence develops, tellers can be encouraged to identify patterns across stories. This development may come from combining the various points of focus and actions or reactions that result in particular unwanted outcomes.

Once these patterns have been identified, it becomes easier for tellers to make conscious decisions about choosing different approaches to practice. Such shifts are not always written in great detail but emerge through dialogue. The focus is on gaining insight, finding alternatives, affirming good practice and exploring a range of responses. What is written are key words or markers from which students can track their reflective thinking.

The stages outlined provide a useful introduction to the reflective process. They enable stories to be told within formal settings where there is a specific focus on gaining insight into the practice experiences. To move students into a conscious reflective mode, it is helpful to place these experiences in relation to theoretical models that explore ways in which learning can develop from practice, and ways in which practice can develop and change through reflective learning. The contributions of Kolb (1984), Gibbs (1988) and Boud, Keogh and Walker (1985) are presented to students at this stage to enable storytelling to be viewed as a reflective activity.

Kolb's (1984) four-step Experiential Learning Cycle consists of concrete experience, reflective observation, abstract conceptualisation and active experimentation. Gibbs (1988) follows a similar approach in the Reflective

Cycle but identifies six stages, and translates Kolb's 'concrete experience into a description of what happens. For students, sharing stories involves becoming connected to the concrete experience and describing what happened. Conversations students have with peers about their stories enable acknowledgement of feelings, evaluation of experiences and often an initial analysis of the situations (Gibbs, 1988). This equates to Kolb's (1984) observation stages, although it may also incorporate something of the reflective phase. Writing and analysing stories enables deeper understanding and themes to emerge which may indicate patterns of behaviour. This phase relates to the analysis and conclusion stage of Gibbs (1988) and the reflection and formulation of abstract concepts (Kolb, 1984). From such insights it is possible to formulate ways in which practice can change, develop action plans (Gibbs, 1988) and test implications (Kolb, 1984).

Boud, Keogh and Walker (1985), on the other hand, examine reflection from within the learning process, which, from their perspective, consists of three key elements: preparation for the experience, the activity, and processing the experience. Each stage involves the affective domain and it is particularly helpful for students to identify how feelings are expressed at each of these stages. This may require storytellers to recall which feelings were present prior to the event, as well as those experienced during the event. Tellers are likely to be most aware of feelings that were present at the end of the experience and those that arise as they are engaged in retelling their story or when they are thinking about their scenario.

When placing the reflective process in context, Boud, Keogh and Walker (1985) identify three key aspects: the experience, the reflective processes and the outcomes. The experience includes not only what is done but also what it is thought about it, the associated feelings and any conclusions that arise as a result. Within this model, the reflective process involves returning to the experience, attending to the feelings, both positive and negative, and re-evaluation. Students have opportunities to re-think an event and make decisions about how it could be different.

While students clearly develop awareness when telling and writing their stories, engaging in debriefing with a small group frequently uncovers further insights. However, an additional reflective step is required to record these insights, new perspectives, ways in which behaviour might be changed, or anticipated outcomes. These phases can be articulated as part of the learning process by extending the previous template so that it is placed on an A3 page.

Title of story:	Focus:	Significant events:
Write your story here:	Key feeling(s) or Key players	
_____	_____	_____
_____	_____	_____
_____	_____	_____
_____	_____	_____
_____	_____	_____
_____	_____	_____
_____	_____	_____
_____ ...	_____ ...	_____ ...

Insight into preparation for the activity:	Processing of experience:	Outcomes:
_____	_____	_____
_____	_____	_____
_____	_____	_____
New insights gained while sharing story		
_____	_____	_____
_____	_____	_____
_____	_____	_____
_____ ...	_____ ...	_____ ...

Key elements that occur are re-evaluation of the experience through recording insights, potential changes to practice and perceived outcomes. It is important to note that not all issues can be easily or immediately addressed. Some issues, such as anxiety related to lack of confidence in performing skills, take time and experience to emerge, and it is even longer before practice develops and changes, which indicates that these aspects are beyond the students' current zone of proximal development. However, through this process students can identify trends in their practice and monitor how their competence is developing. A story from a first-year student is presented to illustrate the process (see Example 1, opposite page).

Awareness gained through internal thought processes and dialogue with peers or mentors enables appreciation and understanding of practice events leading to insights that can advance practice. Once confidence is gained it is possible to move to a less prescriptive and delineated process. While it remains helpful to identify key players, feelings and significant events, emphasis is on tracking patterns of professional behaviour. Insight into these patterns can enable in-depth exploration of what is happening and why, and lead to selecting alternative approaches.

For this stage it is useful to retain the A3 page and ensure it allows plenty of space for writing and analysing stories in addition to comments, additions, amendments and insights.

Such a template could look something like this:

Title of story: *Write your story here:*	*Key players*	*Feelings*	*Significant events*
———————————	————	————	————
———————————	————	————	————
———————————	————	————	————
———————————	————	————	————
———————————	————	————	————
———————————	————	————	————
——————————— ...	———— ...	———— ...	———— ...
Insights from processing:			

Example 1

| *Title of story:* **Chasing My Tail** | *Focus:* Feelings | *Significant events:* |
| | | |

Write your story here:	*Key feeling(s):* Anxiety Relief, Concern	Giving injection Missing patient concern
It was only my second day on the ward, I was really nervous. I knew I would be expected to give an injection – my first. How was I ever going to manage? First thing in the morning – it was only 7.30am – the lecturer came and said that my patient needed an injection. I was so nervous.	Anxiety plus plus!	New experience
However I got the chart, checked and rechecked. Correctly prescribed, correct drug, date, time, dose – I knew it off by heart. The lecturer helped and checked the drug with me. Finally I was on the way to the patient. I went in and explained that I had her injection. I pulled the curtain, asked	Nervous	Focus on myself
her to roll over, selected the site and gave the injection. It all went very smoothly – what a relief. I entered it into the register and on the chart. I had done it. I went back 20 minutes later to check how she was. She was	Elated at success	Focus on getting technique right
still on her side and when I went round beside her I noticed she had the occasional tear falling down her cheek. I froze inside – what had I done! I sat down beside her and asked what was wrong. She explained that she was really worried about her cat. She had only been admitted yesterday	Sick inside	Missing that the patient was upset
and her neighbour was going to see if she could find it and feed it but she hadn't heard and it had been such a cold, wet night. The neighbour was coming in at visiting time and it would get sorted then.	Relief it was OK – but a lingering concern	Relief that she was going to hear later

Insight into preparation for the activity:	Processing of experience:	Outcomes:
Focus on my anxiety and new procedure. Did not think about the patient. *New insights gained while sharing story:* When telling the story I realised that I could have gone and rung the neighbour to find out if the cat was OK. I could have stopped her being worried all morning – she didn't have to wait until visiting to find out.	I am now thinking that there is another step I should have taken. If I had gone to the patient first – before I started to get organised for the injection I could have focused on her first – rather than staying focused on me. I could easily do that, I just need to think ahead – perhaps 5 minutes before an injection is due, I could go and check the patient.	1. Realise how much my anxiety about getting tasks right impacts on my ability to care for others. 2. I will go and check the patient before starting procedures to let them know what I am going to do, but also see how they are. 3. When patients are worried I need to think of ways they can get the information they need more easily – like I could phone family or friends for them.

Example 2

Title of story: Learning the ABC *Write your story here:*	Key players	Feelings (of student)	Significant events
It was my very first school and I was so excited. I was assigned to this class of Year Three children for the first four periods each day. I had talked so much with my friends about the kinds of things I would see – I was going primarily to observe. I guess I was also a bit nervous. Anyway, on the second day I was in the class, the teacher asked me to help her at reading time. I was quite excited. She asked me to sit with one child who was quite a long way behind the other kids. I was to discuss the pictures with him, and encourage him to read. The session went really well and when the play bell went the child's mother came into the classroom and saw me with him. She was thrilled that he was getting extra help and came over to join us. She wanted to know all about the session and what I was doing. We chatted for a while and I was telling her about all the things we had learnt at college. The teacher joined us eventually and didn't seem too happy. I don't know what her problem was. The mother asked the teacher if I could work with her child for the rest of the time I was in the class, but the teacher said there were other things I had to do. I don't know what I did wrong. I really felt as though I had stepped on her toes. I mean I was only doing what she asked and helping the child.	Student Class of Children Teacher [Child with difficulty – added at the end] Mother	Excited Anxious Nervous Excited Confident Pride Excited (to be recognised as a teacher) Deflated Disappointed Frustrated	Beginning in classroom Engaging in actual teaching activity Successfully working with child Engaging with mother of child Teacher intervention – seemed cross Mother's request Teacher's refusal (seemed like a power game)

Insights from processing:

1. I realised that I had not chosen the child as a key player and that concerned me. I didn't think that would ever happen. I was so concerned about the teacher and the way she treated me. That has really caused me to think about the whole situation again.

2. I was surprised to think about the mother as having such a passive role. That never occurred to me when the whole thing was happening. I think I would want that to be different in my classroom.

3. Things changed between the teacher and me when I talked to the mother. I guess she felt I overstepped the mark. I don't think I did but I think she felt threatened. I guess I have to attend to the teacher's feelings in this situation as well as the reactions of the kids and my own feelings.

4. I had never thought of the power play that can go on with teachers in the classroom. Teachers have a lot of control over who is listened to, who gets attention and extra help. I hadn't thought about the power aspect. I will need to think again about what I do in the classroom.

Through such telling, writing and analysis of stories, practice events can be more clearly understood. Through developing conscious awareness of practice stories it becomes easier for students to select appropriate aspects that can be used in the construction of exemplars to illustrate various points of view or theories, or to demonstrate understanding of particular processes.

LEARNING TO WRITE EXEMPLARS AS ASSIGNMENTS

An exemplar is a creative piece of work that is based on experience. Various aspects of personal experience are chosen to illustrate specific points requested in, and required by, an assignment. So writing an exemplar involves documenting the whole or parts of a story or stories in particular ways for specific purposes. There is considerable difference between reflective writing for learning and writing exemplars as part of an assignment.

The purpose of using stories within assignments must be made clear to students, with instructions provided on how to approach the task and provision for them to receive feedback on their attempts. Sometimes this proves difficult and the translation of learning from practice into theory is too complex. Engaging in more formalised storytelling sessions where experiences are shared with educators or peers can provide appropriate backgrounds from which students can identify examples which they can use to illustrate particular learning outcomes. Once these examples have been clarified it is possible for students to provide evidence that outcomes have been achieved.

For students to be able to identify the purpose of a particular exemplar it is essential to have the expected outcomes of the assignment clearly outlined. Examples of requests for exemplars follows.

- Use an exemplar to discuss two of Benner's (1984) domains.
- Demonstrate an understanding of the relevance of the Reflective Processes outlined by Boud, Keogh and Walker (1985), using exemplars to illustrate your discussion.
- Identify four issues involved in an initial assessment of a client. Justify your choice and illustrate with exemplars.
- Discuss three practice competencies and illustrate your understanding through exemplars.

Exemplars require stories to be shaped in particular ways to meet stated outcomes. The shift from reflective incident and reflective processing to writing exemplars requires very specific processes to occur.

1.   Initial engagement in reflective processes to gain insight into practice.
2.   Careful examination of the assignment topic to enable clear articulation of the outcomes required.
3.   Prudent choosing of evidence from experience to best illustrate assessment requirements.

This final process may require simplification of practice examples. Usually this involves choosing to focus on one small part of a larger event or omitting aspects that are not considered appropriate or necessary to illustrate the points that have been decided on in relation to an assignment. This is a complex process and frequently too much information is excluded and the point of the story is lost. Alternatively too much information can be provided and the central issue lost. It is always useful to examine completed exemplars to identify if the key issues are clearly addressed and sufficient background information is provided, while checking to ensure that the main point in a complex scenario is not lost. Constructive feedback is particularly helpful and should be encouraged from peers and available as formative assessment from educators. Constructive feedback will help students understand the process of using stories to demonstrate their practice, and inform their decision-making and discernment in relation to exemplars. In the next chapter we explore the *story expanding* stage in more depth and outline how we encourage students to embrace a reflective approach to practice.

7 Expanding Stories through Reflection

Stories provide us with unique glimpses into practice settings. When we work with stories we can reflect on what has happened in these settings and gain insight into why events evolved as they did. Stories also offer us opportunities to explore alternative approaches to practice. Through thoughtful appraisal of our options, practice can develop. The reflective process provides a particularly useful way to appraise such options. In this chapter we focus on its role in *story expanding,* the third stage of our Reflective Learning through Storytelling Model. We begin by examining the 'what' and 'how' of reflection as it relates to storytelling, then explore ways in which deeper insights can be achieved. To maximize gains from reflection, we also encourage tellers to consider the contexts in which stories are shared and to discuss how storytelling pathways can be used. In addition, we outline how we involve students in meta-analysis, placing particular emphasis on how subsequent learning impacts on practice.

EXPLORING REFLECTION

Examining stories in relation to reflective literature enables students to develop a deeper appreciation of their experiences and the learning they gain as a result of their reflective endeavours. While a significant amount has recently been written on reflection as a concept, it is frequently complex and difficult to apply (Moon, 1999).

As Atkins and Murphy (1993) state, there is no agreed definition although most definitions incorporate some focus on 'thinking' about experience.

We are using the term reflection in two senses. First, the process or means by which an experience, in the form of thought, feeling or action, is brought to consideration, while it is happening or subsequently. Secondly, deriving from the first, the creation of meaning and conceptualization from experience and the potentiality to look at things as other than they are (Brockbank and McGill, 1998: 56).

Reflective learning is a process of internally examining and exploring an issue of concern, triggered by an experience, which creates and clarifies meaning in terms of self, and which results in a changed conceptual perspective (Boyd and Fales, 1983: 99).

. . . reflection seems to be a form of mental processing with a purpose and/or an anticipated outcome that is applied to relatively complicated or unstructured ideas for which there is not an obvious solution (Moon, 1999: 98).

While these definitions refer to some type of processing of experience, viewed as thinking about, mulling over or pondering on, essentially reflection involves attending to events that have been brought to consciousness for re-examination. The depth of thinking required varies considerably. For some events, resolution is found quickly – almost immediately the examination occurs. Other practice dilemmas are more difficult to resolve and require significant formalised processing. These differences suggest a processing continuum in terms of the amount of time and work required. It is also helpful to recognise that examination of practice events, even after initial insight is gained, can lead to further gains.

Moon (1999) attempts to address the differences in definition by highlighting key elements that are 'commonly used' or are part of a 'common sense' understanding of reflection. Her definition uses 'mental processing' to define the thinking that addresses troublesome practice events. Generally such processes are viewed as thinking about, mulling over or pondering on, but essentially reflection involves attending to events that have been brought to consciousness for re-examination. The depth of thinking required varies considerably. Some practice dilemmas are difficult to resolve and require significant formalised processing. However, other events are resolved quickly – almost as soon as examination occurs – or solutions just 'pop up' when there is not conscious awareness of thinking about what can be quite complex situations. While Moon (1999) suggest that the concept of intuition can assist in understanding this phenomena, it is possible that some form of unconscious processing could also be present. Boud, Keogh and Walker (1985) acknowledge the role of unconscious processing but consider it helpful if this comes to consciousness so that the impact on decision-making and learning can be recognised. Unconscious processing needs, in some way, to become part of the complex cognitive processing required when students encounter practice events for which they have no obvious solutions. A useful initial approach to such processing is to focus on the affective elements embedded in events.

The place of feelings and emotions, irrespective of whether they are negative or positive, is important in any reflective process (Boud, Keogh and Walker, 1985). The stronger the emotional content, the more likely it is that stories will be told, and, through telling stories, opportunities created to explore these emotions. The degree to which they are successfully addressed will have a significant influence on the learning outcomes students achieve. When the full range of emotions experienced within any given event is recognised, and integrated with other aspects of stories, it is more likely that insights will be gained. Lack of attention to strong emotions evoked by experience is likely to result in stories that become stuck in the cathartic storytelling conundrum. Repeated tellings for cathartic release do little to resolve underlying issues and are unlikely to inform future practice. However, through acknowledging and integrating affective reactions, within and around stories, it is possible for students to move to processing practice events reflectively in constructive ways.

REFLECTION IN PRACTICE

It is useful for students to identify where reflection fits within practice settings. Schön's (1983) differentiation between the high hard ground and swampy lowland is particularly helpful. The high hard ground in the practicum setting enables theory to be related to practice. Skills can be acquired and problem-solving approaches or technical thinking (Kemmis, 1985) can be applied. Such firm ground enables competence and confidence to develop. Students' stories from these settings are likely to focus on the excitement of learning new skills, the difficulty of gaining the physical dexterity required, the complexity of multi-staged tasks or the anxiety related to putting them into practice in less controlled settings. The reality is that students frequently learn initial skills in controlled settings such as laboratories, the high hard ground. While these are good places for technical learning, they are not where practice occurs. Practice settings are frequently less stable.

In the early days of gaining practice experience it is easy for students to have empathy with the concept of swampy lowlands where there is a constantly changing landscape and contextual features distract attention from specific goals. Within such settings it is necessary to move beyond technical thinking to incorporate the more holistic approach of practical thinking (Kemmis, 1985). This shift enables interpretation of contextual features from practice settings, judgements about the best way to proceed, and evaluation regarding the appropriateness of actions to occur simultaneously. Because choices need to be made and options examined, dialogue and negotiation are essential. Every situation is different and it is important to monitor the relevance of interventions. Such monitoring can occur through reflection, and access to the complexity of the events can take place through stories.

Schön (1983) describes the different ways such reflection occurs. From the perspective of the swampy lowland it is comparatively easy to recognise reflection-in-action where the focus or aim of practice tasks shifts because unforeseen contextual factors impinge. Students can experience a sense of relief when such divergence is seen as a type of reflection rather than an unplanned, uncoordinated approach to practice where key tasks are reprioritised in response to unexpected events! It is useful for students to examine how useful or appropriate any shifts in key tasks have been. On many occasions successful outcomes affirm their decisions. However, at times, confusion, uncertainty or dissatisfaction indicate the need for further exploration and therefore reflection-on-action. This type of reflection depends on students being alert to ever-changing practice contexts, valuing and affirming intuition, and drawing on past experience to explore the relevance of learning to current practice. Relevance is only discovered if thoughtful evaluation occurs.

Reflection-on-action provides opportunities for students to have another look at situations. They can return to experiences, examine them in more depth, explore options and choose alternative actions. Storytelling is a useful way to engage in this type of reflection. Sometimes stories are told with specific issues in mind, but on other occasions, motivation comes from a general feeling of unease or because students feel significant emotional involvement. Stories may be shared within the contexts in which events occur in a relatively informal way or as opportunities arise. For some students, reflection occurs while they are walking or when writing in a diary or journal. On occasions such activities do not provide clarification and more formalised reflective processes need to be pursued to gain some level of resolution (McDrury and Alterio, 2001). Such processes enable stories, based on practice events, to be explored with peers or through semi-structured conversations with educators. Insights gained through reflection-on-action are then available for use through reflection-in-action.

For both reflection-in-action and reflection-on-action there are some fundamental skills to nurture in students. Atkins and Murphy (1993) have collated a list of five key requirements:

- **Self-awareness** is important when naming and processing the feelings related to an event, but also required when examining 'how the situation has affected the individual and how the individual has affected the situation' (p. 1190). Reflective processes expose the interrelations between people and events within the specific contexts.

- **Description of the events** is essential and can be encouraged through storytelling. For some students this will involve verbal sharing but for others it may occur through writing or drawing. It is important that sufficient detail is provided to enable events to be recaptured. Dialogue is an important adjunct to the telling as details are frequently revealed when aspects of stories are being expanded. In the process of such dialogue it is also quite common for 'forgotten' details to be remembered – details that often lead to significant insights.

- **Critical analysis** is important because it involves examining the relevance of '. . . existing knowledge, challenging assumptions and imagining and exploring alternatives' (p. 1190). Within storytelling and reflection it is important that such analysis of stories is not critical in terms of fault-finding or blaming, but rather focuses on gaining understanding and exploring possibilities and alternative options.

- **Synthesis** is required to ensure that there is 'integration of new knowledge with previous knowledge' (p. 1190). Creativity is particularly important in this process as it allows for new perspectives and lateral thinking to be incorporated into the problem-solving equation. Such synthesis is an important aspect of any formal reflective or storytelling process.

- **Evaluation** involves 'the making of judgements about the value of something' (p. 1190). This phase enables students to review the actual and potential outcomes from practice events or the reflection on them, and make conscious decisions regarding future actions.

Self-awareness and the ability to describe events carefully are skills that can be encouraged through professional development. The equally important skills of critical analysis, synthesis of knowledge and evaluation are more challenging. Development of reflective strategies is one way to foster these skills. Not only can these skills be examined and implemented using formal storytelling processes; it is also possible to demonstrate how they can be successfully integrated into practice.

THE REFLECTIVE PROCESS AND STORYTELLING

Many authors agree upon three stages in the process of reflection (Atkins and Murphy, 1993). These are now considered from a storytelling perspective.

- The first stage has been identified as inner discomfort (Boud, Keogh and Walker 1985), or surprise (Schön, 1983). Equally common is an intangible 'something' that makes a situation memorable, 'something' that causes students to ponder about an event. A feeling of something being unfinished, not quite right or unexplained is present. For some reason the event comes to the forefront of consciousness again. It is remembered in its own right, or memory of it is triggered by something else in the environment – another event or another story. When events are not easily accessible or there is difficulty in finding ways to tell stories, it is useful to move to creative ways of representing the events. Drawings, collage, poetry and journalling can assist students to present complex realities. The range of options is endless and it is important to encourage use of these tools so students can reflectively access practice realities.

- The second stage is the working phase where events are examined in detail. This is when stories are told. When creative tools have been used, they become the focus from which stories are shared and dialogue is formed.

    Many authors have explored the processes of critical analysis that occur at this stage (Atkins and Murphy, 1993; Boud, Keogh and Walker 1985; Mezirow, 1981). Such analysis ensures that time and space are created to explore what is known about events. From this analysis the shape and form of stories can be examined, and frequently tellers become aware of connections with other events or discern aspects of their stories that have been unconscious.

    It is also beneficial for some type of formal processing to occur. The actual form it takes appears to be less important than the opportunity to move to a position where, through some type of dialogue, other possibilities are considered. One useful element at this stage is for tellers to be introduced to multiple perspectives of their stories. How would their story look to the other key players, would they interpret events differently? However, insight does not always occur, and the greater the level of unacknowledged or unresolved emotion in relation to stories, the more difficult it is for students to gain insight into other perspectives.

If tellers' feelings are primarily related to their current settings, it is possible to appreciate and value their depth and create the necessary space for new insight by focusing on these feelings and ensuring that the storytelling process encourages their articulation. However, when such feelings link with unresolved issues from the past, it is necessary to return to previous experiences as a point of reflection, in addition to dealing with present issues. Positive outcomes from reflective story-telling processes will only be possible when links and interconnections between past and present are consciously available. Through this process, learning which brings insights can occur and be considered in relation to current practice.

- The third and final stage in the process of reflection relates to outcomes. While various authors have articulated this in differing ways (Boud, Keogh and Walker 1985; Mezirow, 1981; Moon, 1999; Schön, 1983), there is agreement that some type of learning or development through critical thinking takes place that enables demonstration of outcomes. This frequently involves a decision to do things differently but it is equally valid to gain knowledge through reflection about why some events had a positive outcome and to identify what can be tried again if a similar situation occurs.

A natural progression would be to provide a formula that would ensure such reflection. In reality reflection is not a linear process: it involves critical thinking, engaging in dialogue, making connections and gaining insight. While there is no single way to engage in reflection, it does seem that sharing stories encourages a reflective process, especially when storytelling is accompanied by dialogue and occurs in formalised settings. This observation brings us to consider why stories are told and how the settings in which they are shared contribute to student learning.

Maximizing storytelling opportunities

It is important to recognise that choices made around storytelling opportunities can have a significant impact on student learning outcomes.

Perhaps the most difficult aspect of making choices is the need consciously to adopt a reflective learning attitude to experience rather than remain with an approach that results in stories being shared primarily for cathartic purposes. The desire to learn from experience comes to the teller's consciousness in a range of ways. There may be a feeling that an experience did not have the desired outcome or that a conversation did not go well. There may be a thought that even though practice choices were in line with theory, there was something missing, something wrong, and that others might do things in different ways. Such awareness can lead to experiences being shared with the hope of gaining a better understanding so that learning occurs and new strategies for practice are formulated.

When practice events that result in significant emotional reactions occur, tellers are likely to engage in *spontaneous storytelling*. Frequently, spontaneous stories are about something that happened recently – maybe only minutes or hours before the telling. It is also likely that these events had specific affective effects on the tellers: maybe humorous, tragic, sad or frustrating. In contrast, *predetermined stories* are those that have been considered prior to the current telling. This consideration involves some type of conversation around the story that may occur internally as students attempt to gain deeper understanding through reflection-in/on-action. This self-talk is an example of intrapsychological processing as identified by Vygotsky (1978). When such pondering occurs through dialogue with others, as typically occurs during reflection-on-action, it involves interpsychological processing (Vygotsky, 1978).

In terms of outcome, the ability to construct new understanding from stories is likely to increase in relation to the amount of processing that occurs around them. Therefore, while some level of catharsis is likely when spontaneous and predetermined stories are shared, reflective learning from predetermined stories builds on insight already gained. Because there has been some level of prior consideration there is also likely to be a greater openness to the various comments and insights offered.

The number of listeners also impacts on storytelling outcomes. However, rather than having a specific effect on cathartic or reflective learning outcomes, listeners are more likely to influence the type of processing that occurs. If one listener engages in dialogue with a teller it is likely that the conversation will provide in-depth analysis of the event, its context and affective components. This analysis provides an additional perspective on a story. If a small group converses about a story it is possible to gain multiple perspectives. The type of processing that takes place is significant, for unless an appropriate formalised setting is provided *response stories* are more likely to occur than *response dialogue* because the listeners will focus on sharing their own experiences rather than attempting to process the teller's story.

The usual setting in which stories are shared is informal because it is the most readily available option. Practice dilemmas are taken to tea, coffee or lunch breaks and shared before or after work with peers. Unfortunately such settings are less likely to provide tellers with desired learning opportunities and can result in practice dilemmas being viewed as insurmountable, as illustrated in the following example.

Susan, a second-year student teacher, felt she had a problem getting children to focus in her class. She shared this experience informally with her peers as part of a conversation over lunch when back at college for a study day: 'I find the kids are really restless, especially after lunch. They wriggle about, play with pencils and paper, whisper to each other and generally don't seem to care what I am talking about. I find it really frustrating but what can I do?'.

Her peers were sympathetic and talked about various factors that might contribute to such restlessness, including possible gender differences – boys being seen as having more difficulty with this problem than girls – and they all had stories of their own about similar issues. While some of their *response stories* related to students being restless after lunch, most were about various groups of students at different times of the day. Susan gained some understanding into the problem and discovered that other students had similar issues, but she did not feel that she was any better equipped to deal with her situation.

Susan retold her story in a formal setting where there were opportunities to examine and explore the feelings she was experiencing: frustration, irritation and, most of all, inadequacy. Through dialogue a range of possible factors were considered. Susan identified three as helpful to her future practice.

- Sitting still and quietly in a warm room after a meal often results in difficulty with concentration. Wriggling and talking can indicate loss of focus and are a symptom as much as a problem.

- Sudden shifts from activity in the playground to sitting still in the classroom are difficult and techniques need to be introduced to support children to learn how to accommodate this change.

- The amount of energy available for focused concentration in the afternoon is usually less than in the morning.

Susan realised that she knew all these things but had never made the connection between her current problem and this knowledge. She 'wondered' with the group about the kind of after-lunch activities that could provide a more focused environment for the children. She asked her peers specific questions: 'What kind of activities do you arrange for the teaching session immediately after lunch?' 'In particular, what adaptations do you make on a hot day when the children are tired?'. While her peers gave their ideas, many of which Susan found helpful, she also engaged in conversation outside the formal group with colleagues at school and her lecturers. These conversations were around the practicalities of creating a more positive classroom environment. The suggestions Susan found herself thinking about most were:

- Plan an after-lunch activity that is relaxing and undemanding for the children so they can go with their natural body rhythm. Maybe have a quiet time after lunch for younger children where they spend a few minutes in a relaxed posture listening to quiet music before they begin other learning activities.

- If children come to the mat together, limit distractions. If they do not need pencils, erasers or rulers these could be left at their desks.

- Ensure the room is cool on a hot day. Open all windows to let in fresh air – or close windows and turn on the air-conditioning – to ensure the room has a good oxygen level.

- Provide adequate space for children to sit, especially on a hot day, as they are more likely to annoy each other if sitting too close together.

Susan decided that she would gradually work through the various suggestions, trying them out and getting more information and feedback from colleagues and peers as the need arose. For Susan, the most significant difference was in her sense of confidence and competence. Rather than being overwhelmed and feeling inadequate, she felt she now had some options.

Opportunities for sharing stories in formal settings enable a more reflective approach to occur but such learning events, when specifically related to experience, can be limited. However, when students are frequently provided with tutorial sessions, these can be utilised for reflective processing. The degree of success is limited if educators move into didactic or teacher-centered information-giving processes that divert the focus away from reflective dialogue and critique. Sometimes students who want quick answers to questions, rather than persevering with the longer, more involved processing of experience, invite such a shift. Such answers tend to involve surface processing that is less likely to impact on practice, while engaging with reflection frequently takes longer but is more inclined to require deep processing.

Therefore, for a setting to be formal, not only does there need to be a place and time set aside, but the setting also needs to be conducive to facilitating reflective processing. We find it helpful to work within a constructivist paradigm and to focus on processes that encourage collaboration with peers and colleagues through conversation. This approach makes it possible to incorporate and elaborate on the contexts of stories. Through dialogue different perspectives can be shared and different approaches to practice explored.

Learning from reflective storytelling

Once there is openness to learning from practice situations, there are two essential elements that have a significant impact on learning outcomes. First, there need to be opportunities for in-depth exploration or critique of practice. This involves reporting, clarifying, examining and placing experiences within wider contexts. Of particular value are opportunities to view events from different perspectives as this enables shifts in perception to occur and assists students to consider a range of alternative options.

Second, the quality of dialogue facilitated around storytelling events significantly impacts on learning. Merely reporting on events, and having little engagement with emotional responses, actions or desired outcomes, is not likely to lead to new insights. It is through dialogue that we make meaning from experience, come to understand our roles within these experiences and construct new appreciations of practice realities.

Third, pathways taken influence the outcomes achieved. Choices available to tellers relate to the type of story, the number of listeners and the settings in which stories are told. These factors impact on the learning outcomes tellers can achieve. While outcomes are many and varied, they can be classified in terms of cathartic or reflective learning. Both can be beneficial to practice. However, when tellers seek reflective learning outcomes it is more appropriate to tell stories in *formal settings*, as *informal settings* are more likely to lead to catharsis. Likewise, the use of *predetermined stories* tends to enhance reflective learning while *spontaneous stories* focus on catharsis. The relationship between the various combinations of choices and outcomes is illustrated in Figure 7.

Figure 7:   Cathartic and Reflective Learning Outcomes Related to Pathway Choices

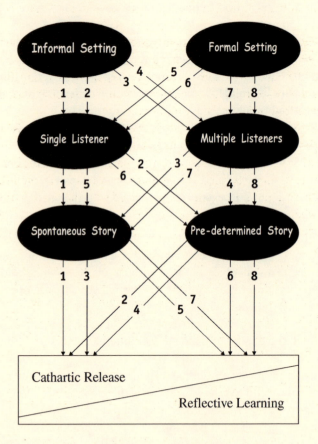

META-ANALYSIS OF REFLECTION

Irrespective of the pathways taken, especially when formal settings are used, reflective storytelling can be approached in many different ways. Reflection can be framed from interpretive (Taylor, 1998), constructivist (McDrury, 1996) or critical social theory (Lumby, 1998; Taylor, 2000) perspectives. In addition, it may be placed within phenomenology (Graham,

1998), grounded theory (Johns, 1998) or action research (Graham, 1998). The approach taken is of less significance than how experiences are processed and what outcomes are achieved through reflection. Processing involves a deepening awareness of practice realities, with the depth and complexity dependent on students' current level of knowledge, stage in the educational programme, personal approach to learning, background and past experience. The outcomes, however, are only evident when changes in behaviour occur or actions become part of practice (Lumby, 1998).

To help students gain insight into reflective processing and the outcomes they achieve, it is useful, at this stage, to provide opportunities for them to engage in meta-analysis of their reflective experiences. Using this process, stories are re-examined to enable the complexity of experience to be acknowledged by identifying various voices.

To examine their experiences reflectively, students scrutinise what they have previously recorded about their practice events. How were they defined? What roles did self and others play? What were the contexts and how were events revealed through actions? Of particular interest are differences about how events are perceived with the passing of time, and those where consistency of perception remains. Consistency is more likely to occur where there continues to be a strong affective reaction to the events.

The place of the teller and others in a story, and the activities that are central to a story, can be further examined by identifying what voices are present. Five levels of voices have been identified in relation to ways of knowing (Belenky *et al.*, 1986) and expanded to be seen in relation to the transformation that occurs through the reflective process (Johns and Hardy, 1998). These are:

- *Silence*: The process of attempting to find a voice; a growth from being silent to finding a voice and being assertive.

- *The Listening Voice*: Received knowledge that focuses on listening to the voices of others, which results in a rigid, unimaginative and narrow perspective where events are prescribed rather than interpreted.

- *The Inner Voice*: Subjective knowledge that involves a quest for self, a knowing of self by gaining an awareness of attitudes and values that are held, concerns that are felt and an alertness about the context within which actions occur.

- *The Voice of Reason*: Procedural knowledge that enables examination and comparison to occur along with a sense of connectedness through which a sense of the whole is retained.

- *Integrating the Voices*: Constructed knowledge that involves the successful integration of information from the various ways of knowing and an ability to incorporate the wisdom of experience into practice realities.

Working with stories in this way involves a three-stage approach that begins with individual work, moves to small group work with three or four students, then provides opportunities for students to record their insights.

The cycle begins with individual work where students select one story from their storytelling file. Such files contain stories that have been previously processed as outlined in Chapter 6, but preferably not recently (as the insights gained are likely to make it difficult to appreciate new understandings which may arise through meta-analysis). A story told and processed at least four or five months earlier is usually ideal.

To reconnect with the story it is useful to engage with the experience by noting the role of self and others, and the details provided about context and the activity. This usually takes about five minutes. It is then appropriate to work with key players in the story and to identify the voices they are using at various times. Frequently this shifts within the story as people relate to other key players. Of particular interest is how different voices are present in particular circumstances or in relation to certain key players.

After working on stories for about 10–15 minutes it is useful to form small groups. In these groups each student has the opportunity to present one key player, identify the voice(s) they are perceived to have had and comment on the impact this has had on the context and activity. Usually insights shared by other students add to those already gained through individual work and it is helpful to have some individual time to record these insights.

Insights gained from such meta-analysis are particularly helpful for students who are using stories as part of their assessment requirements as they enable a further level of understanding of both the event and the reflective process itself.

Using stories to demonstrate reflective outcomes

Outcomes from such storytelling events can be utilised to demonstrate that learning has occurred. This learning frequently happens through the provision of exemplars that relate to practice. While we have previously outlined guidelines for writing exemplars, it is also useful to consider the relationship between assessment and reflection. The writing of practice stories is part of a reflective process that focuses on learning, gaining further insight and exploring how practice can be improved. Such stories are personal reflections that contain positive and negative feelings and practice examples. The primary purpose is to explore an event to enable understanding of it to develop. If reflections are presented for summative assessment, where the focus is on making evaluative judgements in relation to identified outcomes, students can feel vulnerable and may not realise what complexities they have revealed.

To help illustrate the interconnections between these two dimensions, it is useful to use the analogy of two lines of a railway track. One line is reflection, the other assessment.

Figure 8:   Interrelationship between Reflection and Assessment

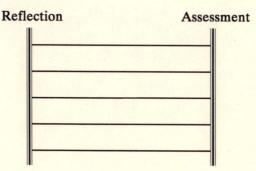

It can be imagined that, with experience, these two elements will merge. However, this is similar to the visual illusion that occurs when looking at a railway track in the distance. The two lines of the track appear to merge – in reality they do not.

Sleepers play an important part for they keep the two lines separate but connected. In terms of reflection and assessment, the separation allows learning and exploration to be distinct from evaluation of outcomes. Through the connectedness it is possible that outcomes revealed while reflecting can be used as part of assessment, and insights gained through assessment may provide direction for future development. Learning and insight can occur while preparing an exemplar just as understanding, appropriate for assessment, can be gained while undertaking reflection. Tools of reflection can therefore be seen as vehicles that travel along the track. Unfortunately this distinction between assessment and reflection is artificial, and it is not unusual for the two to become confused. Reflective pondering is presented in place of insights gained, and summative judgements are made when learning in still in process. Clear distinctions between engaging in learning and demonstrating outcomes is essential.

To facilitate this process it is helpful if tellers are encouraged to keep written stories along with associated reflections in a file, as this enables easy access not only to current stories but also to those that may have been forgotten. These earlier stories can provide examples of development that are particularly helpful when writing exemplars. In addition, new insights can be gained when re-reading, and such reflection is likely to impact on subsequent practice. Such ongoing development illustrates that stories are never fully told, nor fully understood. However, they can be used not only to enhance learning but also to demonstrate learning. Writing stories using exemplars provides a vivid way of demonstrating outcomes or theory–practice links.

Specific learning from stories is enhanced further when reflective processes are provided within formalised settings. In the next chapter two such processes are outlined. The first involves a single listener in a formal setting telling a predetermined story. The second engages tellers in spontaneous drawing prior to storytelling, thus ensuring that some degree of reflection has occurred.

8 Processing Practice Stories

Storytelling, when combined with reflective awareness, provides opportunities for students to gain new insights into their practice experiences. When they share stories in formalised ways they are able to decide which aspects they will reveal. Storytellers' conscious and unconscious choices provide shape to their stories. While key players are frequently introduced, often little attention is given to their background or perspectives. Thus their impact, and the insights they afford, are rarely appreciated in initial tellings. Developing awareness of other ways in which stories can be comprehended further enhances reflective understanding.

Making choices about the settings in which stories are told also influences the reflective learning potential of storytelling. To maximise learning opportunities it is necessary to make conscious choices about when, where and how stories are shared. This will enable better understanding of both the detail of practice events and the many complexities that impact on them.

In this chapter our focus is on the shape of stories, ways of telling them and *story processing*, the fourth stage in our Reflective Learning through Storytelling model. Two formalised storytelling processes are introduced. In the first process a story is shared in ways that enable the teller and listener to explore issues, patterns and themes. The second process begins with spontaneous drawing, which allows students to focus on the congruence between their drawings and the stories they tell about them. In both processes dialogue is central to gaining a reflective perspective on practice. By talking through actions, reactions, thoughts and feelings it is possible for students to uncover alternative interpretations of events and explore various practice options.

SHAPING STORIES

While stories from practice reveal a wide range of experiences, they have some common components (McDrury, 1996). First, there is an 'other' who is the focus and it is always interesting to ascertain who this person is. It could be anyone who is part of the teller's world, such as a student, client, colleague or manager. The 'other' can also be a collective such as a family, a class of children or a group of educators. When this type of grouping occurs it is usual to present the collective as having one voice, attitude and approach.

Second, tellers identify their collaborative processes with the 'other'. It is quite common for this description to include information about affective aspects of relationships, but more unusual for it to focus overtly on power issues. However, power issues are frequently presented in subscripts where tellers present the 'self' of their stories. Such issues may be revealed during dialogue on stories.

Finally, particular issues or themes are presented as the 'action' aspects of stories. While used as a focus point, primarily they provide details and examples of the relationships between key players. They can also enable problems or concerns to be voiced. How these elements are constructed changes with experience and with the unfolding shape of stories viewed as relevant to reflective development. When students are new to a reflective approach, their focus is frequently on 'self' and their stories provide a way to share events primarily as personal experiences. Events are frequently perceived as 'things that happened to me'. There is almost a sense that the stories would have happened anyway – the tellers just happened to be there. The focus of this type of telling is on what happened and is frequently presented as an objective reality – 'this is what happened'. Usually there is minimal awareness by tellers that they could have influenced what occurred. Little thought is given to how events might have looked to others, what they may have perceived or even how their reactions, feelings or attitudes influenced the situations. The tellers' perspectives are paramount and shape such stories. It is difficult to achieve a reflective outlook when stories are told from such viewpoints.

With storytelling experience, the focus shifts from the tellers' perspective to the events that occurred. This shift enables actions to be described in detail and usually includes everything that was said and done. In addition, it can incorporate elements from contexts that influenced the stories. This may include introducing other people who were involved in the scenarios and explaining how they impacted on the activities or outcomes and generally influenced the shape of the stories.

As competence and confidence with both storytelling and practice develop, tellers will spend more time exploring the influence of context on stories and how it impacts on the 'other'. In particular, tellers are likely to see themselves as part of the context and will explore how differences in their actions or reactions could change the dynamics. Such a holistic perspective of events enables tellers to become aware of ways in which stories can change depending on the purpose of the tellings or the contexts in which they occur (McDrury, 1996).

Once tellers develop an awareness of how purpose and context impact, it is possible for stories to assume new shapes. It is likely that a number of people will be involved in all stories. Prior to applying a reflective approach to storytelling, students frequently assume that all the people they have identified in their stories have experienced the recalled events in the same way. They expect them to have the same set of 'facts', think they will have established similar purposes for actions and even see similar outcomes. The reality is that key players are likely to have different versions of events because of the range of affective responses they each experience and the various communication patterns involved as their stories unfold. In addition, their levels of confidence and competence, together with their range of past experiences, influence how events are perceived. Each of these four issues will now be explored in more detail.

- *Feelings and reactions* to events colour stories. It is usual for reactions and feelings to change as events unfold. Stories often reveal situations that begin in positive ways but change direction when things go wrong; the teller ends up feeling disappointed, angry or frustrated. These shifts in feelings effect what happens. They may cause things to be said or done that would not have otherwise occurred. They may cause things to be left undone that would otherwise have happened. In addition, perceptions about the outcomes of stories influence how entire incidents are perceived. The strength of emotions is particularly important as the stronger they are the more significant their impact.

  It is therefore important to address feelings and emotions at the beginning of reflective storytelling processes because making them overt enhances awareness of how they influence events within stories. Becoming aware of the events that cause shifts in affective responses is a key component of reflective practice as it enables patterns of actions and reactions to be identified.

- *Patterns of communication* are another key factor in understanding what is happening within stories. Who is talking, who is listening, and what is being listened to? Examining these aspects enables students to reflect on the roles and relationships of various key players and relate them to their activities. Of primary importance is developing awareness of the interplay between the type and style of communication and the feelings or emotions within stories.

- *Competence and skill levels* in relation to activities, influence perceptions. However, it is the level of experience that enables adaptation of skills to meet changing realities that is particularly important. This ability frequently parallels communication skills, as the capacity to explain, clarify, seek further information or check out shared meanings is an integral aspect of the reflective storytelling process. Once again it is helpful if students are aware that by listening to other students' stories they can increase their own competence and skill levels.

- *Past experiences* of key players is another influential aspect. Perhaps one of the most interesting effects regarding interpretation of stories is the philosophical position of key players. For professionals this is strongly influenced by their academic education, where particular world views are shared through professional knowledge and reinforced through skill development. There may be an underlying perception that the worldview adopted is in fact the best, the right or, in some cases, the superior perspective. Paying allegiance to world views is an important element in remaining an effective member of particular professions such as teaching and nursing.

Clients also come with world views and past experiences. How much they share, what they tell, and how they tell it are all influenced by what is seen as important in current settings. Misreading what needs to be shared, how and when, is a common problem. The professional advocacy role, the process of checking out levels of understanding and asking naive questions, are all important aspects of professional relationships.

With our reflective storytelling approach, we focus on making worldviews overt. While retaining personal perspectives and attempting to appreciate differing philosophical positions of key players, students begin to realise how this information shapes their perceptions of events. When working with others to achieve common goals, part of the challenge is to find ways to acknowledge the strengths of different perceptions.

Keeping these factors in mind, we examine what is brought to and shared within storytelling sessions in the following diagram.

Figure 9:   Individual and Shared Perspectives of Storytelling

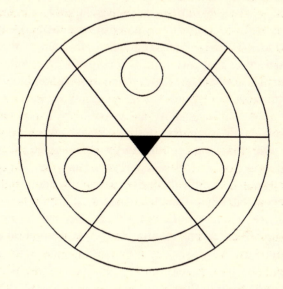

The three small circles represent key players in a story. The inner large circle that encompasses them indicates the setting or context in which a story occurs. It is in this circle that communication is shared and feelings experienced. The outer circle represents past experiences and the philosophical and cultural backgrounds players bring to a story. The wedges indicate how these aspects shape individual perceptions. The black triangle at the centre indicates which aspects of a story are held in common – the parts of a story all players agree have occurred.

The story that is shared represents a particular view of events. Each key player could tell a different story. To advance students' reflective understanding it is necessary to develop their awareness of how meaning can shift when events are viewed from different perspectives.

SHARING STORIES

Students engaging in reflective storytelling opportunities often ask if they need to work with individuals who have similar backgrounds. While it is important for tellers and listeners to establish trust and communicate freely, we consider three issues worthy of mention.

- If listeners and tellers share similar backgrounds it is more likely that real events will be disclosed (Casey, 1998), listeners will be empathetic and there will be a shared understanding of the dilemmas presented by tellers. However, because of the shared experience, and to some degree a shared socialisation, it is more difficult for listeners to present alternative perspectives that encourage tellers to move beyond their current positions. Therefore, it is essential to introduce activities that encourage lateral thinking.

- If listeners do not share similar professional backgrounds to tellers, it is more likely that aspects of the story will be omitted or amended and it will become a cover story (Casey, 1998). However, if the reality were revealed, it could be difficult for listeners to fully understand the events being recounted. While it may be easier for listeners to present different perspectives, it can be difficult for them to provide alternatives that are helpful for tellers and that fit into their philosophical and cultural background.

- Everyone involved in storytelling processes must want to gain insight into practice through reflection. This is a crucial consideration because individual involvement in storytelling may come from different motivations. Some desire catharsis, while others might wish to increase personal understanding of events and participate in order to learn what evolves by sharing insights with others. Frequently there are mixed motivations, but the desire for insight into events is particularly important if maximum gains are to be achieved.

Apart from the degree of homogeneity, being aware of storytelling pathways can assist students to make choices that enhance the likelihood of achieving reflective learning outcomes. These pathways provide tellers with choices about how, when and with whom they can share their stories. Their desired outcome will influence which pathways they choose. While cathartic outcomes are rarely voiced, or even reach consciousness, desire for reflective learning outcomes is usually conscious and stems from a need to gain deeper understanding, find alternative approaches or develop insights into practice events.

To achieve reflective outcomes, tellers need to choose storytelling pathways which have formal rather than informal settings. These *formal settings* need to provide students and educators with opportunities to set aside time and space to examine stories in detail. They are places where experience can be shared and where, through dialogue, it is possible to gain insights or explore alternatives that extend practice.

Reflective learning can be further enhanced if events have been processed in some way prior to telling stories about them in *formal settings*, because their shape and content evolves as they are pondered on or shared. Even when stories are told for cathartic purposes or written about in journals and some understanding is gained, subsequent learning, available in formal settings through formalised storytelling processes, can build on these gains.

Dialogue focused on stories being shared is an essential ingredient in achieving reflective outcomes. It can take a range of different shapes depending on which formal process is used and how many listeners are present. With one listener there are opportunities to focus on events in depth, while multiple listeners make it possible to achieve breadth. However, the number of listeners is less important than the opportunity to gain personal insight into actions and develop an appreciation of alternative perspectives. When reflective endeavours fail it is often because there was too much reliance on particular tools such as storytelling, journalling or drawing, and insufficient focus on dialogue.

It is therefore helpful to separate the use of tools from the reflective processes contained within dialogue. The following diagram provides a visual representation of the interrelationship of the various aspects.

Figure 10:   Interface between Events, Tools and Dialogue

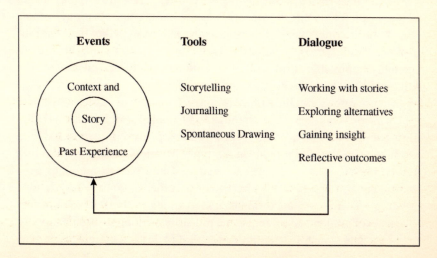

We depict the three phases of this process as *event, tool* and *dialogue*. The *event* involves the context and past experience (outer circle) and the story itself, with a particular focus on patterns of communication and feelings of the teller (inner circle). The *tool* can involve a range of approaches that are primarily vehicles to make an event available for discussion. *Dialogue* is the process of working with stories to enable critique of practice and identification of implications for practice. This final stage is the key component of formal storytelling and an essential aspect of reflective learning.

INDIVIDUAL WORK WITH STORIES

Working with stories in formalised ways provides tellers and listeners with opportunities to have in-depth conversations about their experiences and to process them in ways which may lead to insight and bring about thoughtful change to practice. To ensure the safety and wellbeing of tellers and listeners throughout reflective processes it is prudent to consider support and confidentiality issues (Alterio, 1998).

It is important to provide safeguards with any formalised reflective storytelling process because participating in such activities can raise disconcerting issues. It is therefore appropriate to provide students with suitable support such as access to counselling or other services (Alterio, 1998). In addition, it is important to deal with issues of confidentiality. While stories clearly belong to tellers, through reflection, listeners are also likely to develop personal insights.

While it is relatively straightforward to ensure that original stories remain with tellers through negotiated agreements made prior to forming storytelling partnerships, listeners may incorporate aspects of their learning from a teller's story into a later telling of their own story, something that is virtually impossible to monitor. This dilemma is discussed in depth in Chapter 10 where ethical issues are considered.

We use one storytelling process in which we record stories and sometimes have them transcribed so they are available for individual and joint reflection. If the cost of transcribing tapes proves insurmountable, a useful alternative is to provide audio-tapes to tellers and listeners so they can re-play their stories between their first and second meetings. Any notes can then be referenced back, using a timer or counter on the tape recorder. This particular formalised storytelling process, which involves one listener and one teller, requires a pre-story meeting to discuss support, confidentiality, story ownership and ethical issues and to agree on taping and transcribing arrangements (Alterio, 1998).

The actual process consists of two meetings: one to tell the story and another to maximise learning through reflective dialogue using the transcript or audio-tape. While the amount of time between these two meetings is flexible, two to four weeks seems to maximise gains. This time-frame allows for the tape to be transcribed or duplicated and for the teller and listener to receive their copies for the purpose of reflecting individually on the story.

This process, which values emotional responses, has four stages. It incorporates oral, written and dialectic reflection and involves individual and joint reflective phases. The teller has full control over which story is told. The story can be *spontaneous* or *predetermined*. A quiet room where the teller and listener can work undisturbed is required, along with a tape recorder and a tape.

Stage 1 – Deciding on a story

The teller may choose any story. This may be one which has already been talked about with friends or written about in a journal. If prior reflection has occurred, the story is classified as *predetermined*. If the teller has difficulty thinking of a story, the listener can assist with key prompts based on Diekelmann's (1990, 1992) work with nurses. Examples of such prompts are:

* Tell me a story, one you will never forget, about something that hap-pened in your practice.
* Tell me a story about something that caused you to rethink and change aspects of your practice.

If the teller comes to the session with several stories and needs to make a choice about which one to tell, the listener can help by asking some key questions, for example:

* Which situation are you most concerned about?
* Are there any common themes or patterns in the situations you have recalled?

At this point it may also be appropriate for the listener to support the teller to develop a plan which accommodates the untold stories in an acceptable way.

Stage 2 - Telling the story

The main focus in this stage is on the story being shared. For individualised formal storytelling to be an effective tool, it is important for the teller to introduce contextual aspects such as locating their story in a specific time and place and describing key players in ways that enable the listener to ascertain their significance. Disclosing and valuing affective aspects also enriches this storytelling process.

It is important for the listener to stay focused on the teller's story rather than introduce new material or making reference to their own experience, regardless of whether it is similar or not. For the listener to be effective in their role, an open non-judgmental listening approach is required. At times the listener may ask clarifying questions, establish facts and, of course, give minimal encouragers such as nods and smiles.

Once the story is told, the teller and listener dialogue about it to uncover layers of meaning and identify alternative perspectives. This may involve statements or questions that seek to clarify content, explore feelings, expand aspects of the story or examine possible solutions or resolutions.

Stage 3 - Reflecting individually

Once the story is transcribed or the tape copied, both the listener and teller receive a copy to enable an individual reflective phase to take place. The teller has opportunities to delete, add or alter any aspect of the story. The transcript or tape often alerts the teller to stories with similar themes or helps the teller to remember forgotten aspects of the current story. The listener also reflects on the written or aural account of the teller's story, identifying any aspects about which they wish to seek further clarification.

Stage 4 - Reflecting jointly

The focus of this second meeting is to reflect jointly on the teller's story. This meeting can also be audio-taped if the teller wishes as it frequently provides dialogue pertinent to developing and changing practice. At this stage, the teller shares with the listener any additions, deletions and alterations they have made or want to make to their script or tape. These are then discussed and their relevance identified. The listener's role is to assist the teller to clarify, explore and expand the story to ensure maximum learning gains can be made. It is also appropriate at this stage for the teller and listener tentatively to explore possible links between aspects of the story and the significance of any themes or patterns that have emerged. For example, there may be links between the roles of key players and their actions. Some actions may reveal power related themes. It is important that the listener uses reflective questioning rather than statements as making these links essentially belongs to the teller and dialogue needs to be focused around the teller's growing insight.

In the final phase of this stage it is important that the teller and listener focus on insights gained. Some stories are resolved at this point in ways that feel complete to the teller and need no further discussion or action. If this is not the case, the teller has opportunities to formulate possible solutions to unresolved issues and to explore, through dialogue, their potential, and the consequences of implementing them. Once the teller is clear about which options to pursue, an action plan is constructed. It is up to storytelling partners to decide if they want to arrange a further meeting to discuss the outcome of instituting the action plan (Alterio, 1998).

Some stories may be re-visited many times, in many ways. Re-negotiation of original storytelling agreements is always an option. Transcripts or tapes of the story may be re-read or listened to several times. Each storytelling pair decides how they want to manage their arrangement.

Formalised storytelling, like purposeful teaching, captures everyday moments and turns them into learning opportunities. The teller's level of openness to viewing alternative perspectives and devising acceptable solutions, together with past experiences and intensity of feelings associated with the story, affect how it is processed and what learning is achieved. In the following example Jim, a male lecturer teaching in a higher education setting in a large cosmopolitan city, recalls how a racial accusation left him devastated. He told his story in response to the key prompt 'Tell me a story about something that happened in your practice, something you'll never forget'.

> It was a dreadful thing, it was to do with race relations. There was a discipline problem where I had to deal with three students from a minority group. I had always worked very hard for this group but I ended up disciplining them. I didn't handle one aspect of it very well although it wasn't intentional. I was accused of racism and a complaint was laid with the Human Rights Commission and Race Relations. Race Relations thought it had been blown out of proportion and wouldn't get involved but it got to a level where the person in the Human Rights Commission dealt with it rather badly. She was taken off the case because she had listened to the three students and not taken into account that there might have been another perspective, mine! I felt like things were out of control. I was being accused of racism despite working very hard for the minority group these three students belonged to and I had given extra to these students to make sure they had the

best opportunities. It impacted quite badly on me. I'm very cautious now in my dealings and I'm almost paranoid about racial jokes. I won't get involved in anything that might put me in that position again so I haven't really come to terms with it.

Jim went on to explain how this experience was only resolved when the Human Rights Commission appointed a different person to the case. This person talked to everyone concerned and came to the conclusion that there was no case to answer. The aftermath of this experience had long-term effects for Jim because he was not offered an apology and was left with unresolved feelings. He talked about learning 'to be cautious' and 'feeling helpless' to defend himself. These feelings were still evident when he shared his story; however, they changed as Jim reflected on and discussed various aspects.

Using the four-stage formalised individual storytelling process described, Jim was able to attend to the three stages of reflection as identified by Boud, Keogh and Walker (1985): returning to an experience, attending to feelings and re-evaluating the experience. This process enabled him to make public his private anxieties and provided him with a safe forum in which to explore them. During the joint reflective phase, he reassessed his role in the incident and decided he had contributed to his feelings of helplessness by becoming defensive. He came to the conclusion that he would benefit from putting some strategies in place to ensure that he did not react to challenging situations in the same way again. Jim described how the storytelling process helped him reach resolution by saying, 'telling my story then seeing it all down in black and white [in the transcript] then discussing what happened and why I still felt so strongly about it enabled me to move on'.

As a result of telling his story and engaging in reflective dialogue, Jim was also able to identify factors that were out of his control, such as the inadequate processes his institution initially followed to investigate the complaint. Letting go his feeling of helpfulness, accepting that, given his level of skills and range of experience at the time, he had done his best, and devising a plan which included having regular supervision so he could manage future challenging situations constructively, were significant advancements for Jim.

Key aspects of this storytelling process demonstrate a constructivist approach to learning. Collaboration between teller and listener is essential, for such relationships rely on trust and commitment. Through conversation meaning is constructed and insight gained, although what the teller and listener learn may differ. The context in which the original event occurred

– the *happening setting* – is recalled and aspects of it are described in the story being told in the *telling setting*. Both contexts are important, for each contributes to the quality of the reflective process.

SPONTANEOUS DRAWINGS

Another effective reflective tool is spontaneous drawing. Already used extensively within psychology and psychoanalysis, it is seen as a tool to aid assessment or as part of a therapeutic intervention. Within a reflective learning context its primary purpose is to enhance learning and encourage professional development. Restricting its use to this purpose requires dialogue primarily focused on the level of congruence that exists between the oral story and the associated drawing.

Using spontaneous drawing as a beginning point for storytelling enables tellers to have a pre-storytelling reflective phase. While drawing, tellers have opportunities to ponder on their stories and this reflection, known as intrapsychological processing (Vygotsky, 1978), can add clarity and focus to the subsequent telling. Such reflection enhances learning potential and increases the likelihood of achieving positive learning outcomes. Spontaneous drawing is particularly useful in assisting students to integrate theory and practice, or to articulate and integrate theory developed from practice. Frequently, such links are too complex or nebulous to be available in other ways. Drawing enables the complexities of practice realities to be brought to consciousness and thus become available to the drawer who is seeking to make connections and associations that will increase insight into practice.

The process of working with drawings, which can appear deceptively simple, is guided by five key principles:

- Drawings belong to the drawer. Ownership is important and to feel safe the drawer must know that they have the right to say what their drawing is about, and what happens to it. Of particular importance is the problem of projection: that is, an unconscious process involving transfer of subjective reality or problem on to an object or person (Jung 1926). When this happens, the subjective reality comes from the person listening to the story, which is told from the drawing, and is projected onto the object or person in the drawing or onto the drawer. There may be elements in a drawing which consciously or unconsciously remind listeners of events from their own past experience resolved or unresolved. Problems are particularly likely to arise if such issues are unconscious and unresolved. It is therefore important that listeners focus on the drawing and the related story but remain aware of their own reactions to it.

- Keep requests for drawings simple. The usual instruction for a drawing is: 'Draw a picture, something you were involved with recently in practice – something that you have wondered about or perhaps a situation where you were not happy with the outcome. Everybody in the drawing must be doing something, no stick figures.' There may be questions about the limitations on stick figures but Furth (1988) identified the importance of looking at the internal consistency of drawings, and stick figures limit the ability to explore this.

  For many who engage in spontaneous drawing there is a feeling of artistic inadequacy. 'But I can't draw' is a common initial response. This need not be a problem as those with artistic ability are likely to bring too much conscious processing to their drawings and the process is therefore less effective. This is frequently followed by 'But what shall I draw?'. Providing a quiet, focused time for processing and keeping the request for a drawing constant are important ways of leaving space for a scenario to emerge.

- Draw from your own experience. It is important that the drawer does this rather than attempting to illustrate something that happened to someone else. If such a situation *is* chosen, the picture needs to be drawn from the perspective of the drawer. How was the story shared, where did it happen, what was shared?

- Share the story from the drawing. The main task of the listener is to attend carefully to the drawing, facilitate the telling, listen to the detail of the story and seek clarification of any aspects of the drawing or story that remain unclear. Of particular focus at this time is the congruence between the story, picture and feelings. What is presented in the picture? What is revealed in the story? In addition, the drawing process itself can reveal to the drawer issues that need to be addressed.

  The reflective phase of drawing, prior to telling the story about it, frequently uncovers issues that need to be addressed or provides possible solutions to dilemmas. These insights are often shared before the story because they become the main focus of the drawer's attention. The insights indicate the reflective learning that has occurred and the story is told by way of explaining what this learning is about.

- Dialogue about the story. The final stage involves the listener 'wondering' about any incongruence that has arisen between the oral story, the drawing and the identified feelings. When learning has already occurred through the process of drawing, dialogue may be minimal.

EXAMPLE

The following drawing was presented by a third-year nursing student. The pre-storytelling reflective phase enabled her to gain insight into an issue that had caused her considerable distress. The student came to the reflective session after a meeting with her clinical lecturer that resulted in her feeling angry and frustrated. She had gone to the lecturer to express her concern and felt that the lecturer had not listened.

Figure 11:   Spontaneous Drawing for a Practice Setting

When asked to share the story from her drawing, the student focused on the insight she had gained. She had realised what had happened in the interview with the lecturer and knew what she needed to do to resolve the situation. She decided she would go back to the lecturer and have a further conversation about the family. The key issue was a rethinking of the definition of abuse the student had used when responding to the educator's questions. When the educator spoke of abuse the student had restricted her interpretation to physical abuse. Through the process of drawing, the student had come to a broader definition that incorporated psychological and emotional abuse.

The story was shared by way of explanation. The student was on a clinical placement in the community providing support for a child with multiple disabilities who was being cared for by her father following the parents' separation. Over a two-week period the student had growing concern regarding the father's behaviour towards another child, his son. The mother, who had initiated the issuing of a non-molestation order against the father to protect the son because of earlier abuse, became frustrated with the boy and dropped him off at his father's front gate. This was done several times and without any prior notification to the father. The mother would then call back several hours later to pick up the boy. During such unplanned visits the father would frequently engage in aggressive verbal outbursts.

The student was unsure what she should do. Should she report the problem? Who deals with such issues? Was it serious enough to worry about? Such questions caused her to go back to the clinical lecturer to explore ways in which her concerns could be addressed.

In this subsequent discussion between the student and the lecturer it was agreed that both parents were abusing the son. Together the student and lecturer notified relevant authorities. The student identified the opportunity to re-explore definitions of abuse as most significant to her learning process.

There are various other ways in which drawings can be used to gain insight into practice. The work of Furth (1988) is particularly helpful in exploring further possibilities. He provides a useful introduction to working with pictures and illustrates how dialogue can be developed further.

The individual storytelling process described in this chapter enables tellers and listeners to focus on events in depth, while spontaneous drawing provides opportunities for students to engage in a pre-reflective phase prior to telling stories. Both processes enhance students' potential to achieve constructive learning outcomes. Telling stories to multiple listeners involves a different reflective process and this is the focus of the storytelling activity outlined in the next chapter.

9 Reconstructing Stories within a Group Setting

Stories provide us with a particular perspective on situations. They also supply information about some of the people involved and reveal aspects of events that occurred. Tellers choose their selection of people and events, often unconsciously, to create particular scenarios or make specific points. To move to more comprehensive understandings of complex practice realities, it is helpful to examine events in greater detail. In this chapter, the socio-cultural perspective (Vygotsky, 1978) is examined further, with specific focus on the impact context has on events and how interaction with others shapes outcomes. To learn from experience, stories that reveal contexts and interactions are explored through dialogue to enable insights to be shared and learning from events to be internalised. *Story reconstructing*, the fifth and final stage of our Reflective Learning through Storytelling Model, is demonstrated using a formalised group-storytelling process.

Facilitation of dialogue and exploration of multiple perspectives is the focus of the group-storytelling process presented in this chapter. This process aims to provide support for all group members and, in particular, the teller. The learning context that results supports the whole group to contribute to collective insights and to develop a deeper understanding and appreciation of professional practice.

A SOCIO-CULTURAL FRAMEWORK FOR STORYTELLING

One significant aspect of socio-cultural theory is that it acknowledges the importance and impact of setting on learning and development. This context for learning, known as the activity setting within Vygotskian theory, defines where higher mental functioning occurs. In particular, the setting determines the degree to which students feel free and motivated to explore and discover (Brown and Reeve, 1985). Tharp and Gallimore (1988) have identified five aspects of the activity setting: who, when, where, what and why.

Activity setting

Who relates to the people involved in a story but, more particularly, focuses on constraints or opportunities that arise because these people, rather than others, are involved. This aspect may be identified in terms of openness or input, but could equally relate to personalities and the way people interact with others. While some of the people who influence the story are obvious because of their roles, others, who are equally influential, may not be so obvious. Family and friends, colleagues and peers or administrators and managers are examples of individuals whose actions and reactions could directly impact on a story. Of particular importance is the fact that some of the most influential people in relation to a story may not have been present when the event occurred.

Such considerations and timeframes are the focus of *when*. Events that are easily accommodated at certain times of the day may be difficult to deal with at other times. The number of people available to assist, the tiredness of individuals involved and the likelihood of other commitments taking priority are examples of the way timing can impact on events. A situation that could usually be resolved in a couple of minutes may take considerably longer if it occurs at a different time of day.

Equally relevant is *where* an event occurs. The ability to contain, maintain or sustain an event, or the people involved in it, is significantly influenced by where it occurs. Dealing with a cardiac arrest on a street corner is quite different from managing it in a ward setting. Engaging in dialogue about animal habitats is a different experience in a classroom and a farm setting.

What is discussed in relation to what is done and not done, along with how something is performed: it enables the identification of behaviour patterns. These patterns can offer interesting insights into the ways in which contexts are shaped by key players in stories. Statements such as 'The children are always so restless when I take the class', or 'The group I take always enjoys music but the other teacher says the children don't enjoy it', or 'When I am in charge something always goes wrong' are examples of identified but not fully processed patterns. It difficult to gain insight by focusing on what has occurred without examining why such actions or reactions eventuated.

Why activities occur is of particular importance as this aspect identifies the degree of goal-directed behaviour. Goals are significant because behaviours will continue only as long as goals are present (Adams, 1994). There are two aspects to consider: motivation and meaning.

Motivation for students to be engaged in activities is related to the perceived desirability and/or acceptability of goals or tasks. Of particular interest is the ownership of goals. In education circles there is a focus on engaging in goal-directed behaviour and encouraging students to be goal directed. However, there are dangers in educators being so goal directed, focused and clear about the direction activities are to take, especially if students do not share the same goals. It is interesting to explore and examine the goals of others and, of course, there will always be both overt and covert goals, with covert goals being more difficult to articulate and the most influential in a given situation. The ideal situation from a constructivist learning perspective is for educators and students to construct goals collaboratively. Care must be taken to ensure that students are actively engaged in constructing goals rather than passively accepting them (Smith, 1988). However, constructing goals does not necessarily mean that everyone fully understands their meaning or implications. It is useful to revisit goals throughout the learning process to clarify, re-negotiate or adjust direction. Perhaps most importantly, failure to achieve goals should always result in serious re-examination of them. How were they set? Who set them? Why were they set and who gains what from achieving them?

Meaning is established gradually and occurs with personal ownership and development of shared meaning of events, known as intersubjectivity (Adams, 1994; Tharp and Gallimore, 1988). At the most basic level this involves an ability to understand and use a shared vocabulary, but also requires an awareness and acceptance of underlying cultural values (Smagorinsky, 1995). Intersubjectivity is central to the whole interpersonal dynamic that occurs in activity settings. It incorporates cognitive and affective components (Ratner and Stettner, 1991) and is therefore an important aspect in successful learning (Tudge, 1991). It is possible that what is thought to be a similar or shared learning experience for students may, because of varied socio-historical and socio-cultural backgrounds, result in very different learning experiences (Manning and Payne, 1993). Language is the fundamental tool to enable achievement of intersubjectivity and common goals in learning. Language is used in conversation with others or when talking to self. The tool of language will shape and form interactions. The type of conversation which occurs between people when learning takes place – the interpsychological process – will be mirrored in the self-talk that happens when students attempt to work through issues on their own – at the intrapsychological level.

Language

Language is used through collaborative interpersonal processes, where students work with someone who is more capable, to achieve a higher level of mental activity than they could achieve alone (Belmont, 1989; Brown and Palincsar, 1986; Smolucha and Smolucha, 1989; Tudge, 1990). Establishing shared meaning is essential. Not only does this allow students to appreciate the depth and complexity of meaning inherent in activities, but it also enables them to express their newly achieved knowledge in appropriate ways.

Students usually spend time, in the initial stages of being introduced to new material, exploring appropriate use of language and specific or technical terms. Trying out new terminology requires that learning remains a social process, as feedback on the appropriateness of language usage is essential. Once students become familiar and confident with the language, they can use it '. . . to monitor personal behaviour and to justify as well as enact personal beliefs' (Spouce, 1998: 262). During these processes there is a gradual shift to the second level of learning, the intrapersonal level (Steward, 1995). Language is gradually internalised, used to express specific technical concepts or internally monitor technical procedures, and provides a frame of reference for complex activities. This frequently involves 'self-talk' that continues until new learning becomes thoroughly integrated. Once fully automated the learning is defined as 'fossilised'. When students engage in a re-examination of material they have known previously, this process is called the 'recursive loop' (Gallimore and Tharp, 1990).

Zone of proximal development

Gauging the appropriate level of support needed by students engaged in collaborate learning processes is complex, especially when working with adults as they usually develop higher mental functioning through their interactions. The gap between what individual students can achieve unaided and what can be achieved under guidance or in collaboration with peers or a more competent other is referred to as the zone of proximal development (Vygotsky, 1978). Providing mutual support for learning creates a bi-directional zone of proximal development. Information is shared, questions that extend comprehension are asked and together this facilitates framing and re-framing of knowledge in ways that are mutually beneficial. While one student is being introduced to new knowledge, another may be gaining new insights, and having understanding refined or deepened.

Being open to such learning opportunities is vital when working with adult students, and is particularly important if embarking on learning through reflection. Irrespective of students' and educators' levels of knowledge, both can learn from each other. The ability to be open to the experience of another, to dialogue about that experience and shape possible future practice, will only work if collaboration within a constructive framework facilitates. The presence of didactic, teacher-centred information changes the dynamic and inhibits learning from experience. However, provision of information that can assist students to structure their thinking or actions can support learning (Gallimore and Tharp, 1990). Such cognitive structuring can help students to organise material and provides the means by which self-evaluation can occur. Such structuring can simply supply a name for something that has happened, label a particular series of events as a whole or provide a broad overview or umbrella from which it is possible to comprehend wider relationships.

Questioning

A more usual way to engage with students in the collaborative learning process is through questioning. Skilled use of questioning is particularly useful as it opens up new possibilities for development and extension of knowledge. Questions can enable students to articulate what is known and this information can be used for two purposes. Firstly it can enable assessment of knowledge, and secondly it can reveal gaps in understanding. While Gallimore and Tharp (1990) differentiate between the types of questions used for each purpose, in our experience with collaborative dialogue, responses to questions provides information that both articulate knowledge and reveal gaps in understanding.

In contrast, through intrapersonal questioning students question their own knowledge or behaviours. Such questions may arise because a theory–practice gap is identified, an unexpected outcome occurs or patterns of behaviour differ from those previously experienced. As an initial response, students scan their existing knowledge and past experiences in search of appropriate solutions. While Schön (1983) identified this process as part of reflection-in/on-action, in socio-cultural theory it is referred to as the 'recursive loop' (Tharp and Gallimore, 1988) where self-regulation, through self-speech or private dialogue, is usually sufficient for students to understand and manage the task.

When students cannot make the necessary links from their own knowledge and experience, the problem shifts from the intrapersonal level to the interpersonal level. If the problem is not too complex or if a specific gap in knowledge is identified, the necessary information is often requested, through specific questions, from more competent peers. However, when the situation is complex, confused or multidimensional, or an informal setting did not provide an environment in which an appropriate response was received, the whole scenario can be shared through telling stories in a *formal setting* that leads to reflection-on-action.

Examining the process enables insight to be gained into the different ways in which reflective learning and reflection through storytelling can occur. Learning is possible when examining situations that are puzzling, new or different, and also when exploring those encounters that are considered familiar and well known. Engaging in reflection through storytelling can provide this additional learning opportunity and involves examination and re-examination of material and active learning in the zone of proximal development. To maximise gains and enhance learning opportunities the process of collaborative dialogue is fundamental, because it is this activity that enables the construction of a new reality through acknowledgement of, and working with, the dialectic.

LEARNING THROUGH STORYTELLING

Fundamental to the concept of the dialectic is the process of moving from differing realities to new realities. This construction may be defined as thesis, antithesis and synthesis (Van der Veer and Valsiner, 1994) but, for our purpose, is more usefully seen in terms of working with different ways of knowing such as cognitive and affect, thought and action, individual and group (Kemmis, 1985). Exploration of these elements within events that are well known, and within tellers' experiences, can enable new synthesis or appreciations to occur. As a result, experiences can be re-situated within different cultural frameworks or perspectives that challenge tellers to develop new ways of knowing and understanding experience which, in turn, can lead to significantly different approaches to practice. However, it is important is to acknowledge the disparateness of various elements and discover ways that dialogue and collaboration can assist in achieving new and often radical outcomes.

The dialectic can be imaged as threads that are plaited together to make a new, stronger entity. The various components are foundational to the new structure and, to some extent, shape outcomes. However, the analogy is limited. Outcomes frequently take on shapes that are quite different from those that could be expected from the initial threads.

When this dialectic is purposefully engaged, there is a shift in focus from the self as the axis of all action and centre of all development, to recognition of multiple players that impinge on change. The action is seen to be embedded not only in personal knowing but also in the collective knowledge of professions, communities and cultures. It involves recognition that others have awareness, insight and different knowledge and can therefore provide alternative approaches and solutions to situations and problems. Developing such awareness is a fundamental aspect of reflection that can, in turn, change practice. This praxis, where critical reflection informs action (Kemmis, 1985), enables action to be informed by theory and grounded in the wisdom and experience that exists within the contexts in which practice occurs.

Consideration of the contexts in which stories occur assists tellers to come to an appreciation of the various layers of meaning that can exist in stories. Incorporating such complexities into processing practice events can be difficult unless a formalised storytelling approach is used. A senior staff nurse working in a paediatric unit shared the following story using a formalised storytelling process.

> I had been caring for a child who had very serious leg injuries, but since admission to hospital had been amazingly settled and accepting of his situation. On the particular day in question this child's dressings were to be changed. I had discussed the procedure with the child and his mother, who was concerned and wanted to be there, so I arranged a convenient time. The mother arrived with two siblings and I began the dressing. Soon after beginning the child became extremely distressed so I provided additional pain relief. This failed to give sufficient cover for the child so I tried all available approaches to make the procedure more comfortable. However I had little success and the dressing was completed but in less than ideal circumstances. I felt frustrated and disappointed that I did not have the skills and ability to deal with this situation.

At the end of the story the nurse engaged in a discussion about the context in which the event occurred. She suddenly remembered that there was a lot of crying going on in the ward at that time. She had not been conscious of it as part of the story but now, thinking back, it was there in the background. It was then that she made the conscious connection that her own son had been to theatre that morning to have minor ear surgery. It had not occurred to her before that this was also part of the context of the story.

Such intrapersonal reflection-on-action can also occur when writing stories in journals or when engaging in personal reflection on stories that have been previously written about. During such reflection students provide their own support for re-framing problems. By re-thinking situations, using their existing knowledge and experience, they arrive at new perceptions of their stories.

When dealing with complex stories from practice, intrapersonal reflection-on-action is frequently insufficient to provide satisfactory reflective outcomes and the additional scaffolding of a formal storytelling process is required. This shifts the process to an interpersonal reflection-on-action. Formalised storytelling is ideally suited for such situations. A formal group-storytelling process that facilitates students to articulate various dialectic dimensions is now outlined.

A FORMAL GROUP-STORYTELLING PROCESS

Three elements underpin the formal group-storytelling process.

- First it is important to value both the range and intensity of affective responses that are part of professional experiences, as they provide important information about the type of engagement in practice (Boud, Keogh and Walker, 1985).

- Second it is useful to explore various perspectives of stories. Essentially a story is told from the teller's perspective, but this can mistakenly be seen as an objective reality, especially if it has been written in a journal or recorded as an exemplar. The stronger the affective involvement, the more likely the perspective is to be seen as 'truth'. Yet others could recount the event in very different ways (McDrury, 1996).

- Finally it is important to consider alternative responses that could be appropriate in such scenarios. Listeners play an important part in this dialogue as they 'wonder' how they might respond to similar situations. Through responses they highlight their perception of events and incorporate a range of professional skills that could be used in such situations. To facilitate such outcomes, good group-processing skills are required (McDrury, 1996).

The number of students in groups is important and while four to eight works well, six seems to be the optimum number. Fewer than four results in insufficient alternative perspectives for the reflective process to work well. When there are more than eight there are too many students to contribute in a focused way. Because of the type of discussion being undertaken, it is important that the group includes a skilled facilitator. The role of the facilitator is to ensure the effective functioning of the group. It is important that this person has trust in, and respect for, the collaborative process and is committed to sharing experience rather than engaging in didactic teaching. The other key role of the facilitator is to maintain the safety of group members, especially the storyteller, for example from projection by other members of the group (McDrury, 1996).

STEPS IN GROUP STORYTELLING

Deciding on a story

When a group initially gathers to share a story it is not unusual for it to take some time for one to emerge. It is important not to rush this stage and that no one feels pressured into having to tell a story. If time allows and the context feels safe, a story will emerge. Once the group is familiar with the process a more common problem is that more than one member of the group will have a story they wish to have addressed. When this occurs it is important that those group members whose story is not used have other ways to deal with their concerns.

Listening to the story

It is important to encourage listeners to attend carefully to the teller and not become focused on creating a *response story* from their own experience. To assist this process listeners are asked to focus on imagining how they would feel if they experienced a similar situation. This process enables them to make conscious a range of affective responses that can occur within such experiences.

It is essential that the group is clear that the story listeners are imagining will be somewhat different from the reality experienced by the teller. What listeners are imagining is their own version or interpretation of the story – their perspective rather than the teller's reality. However, there are likely to be sufficient similarities to enable the teller to gain insights from the listeners' perspectives. At the end of the sharing process it is appropriate to provide opportunities for the teller and listeners to clarify misinterpretations or areas of confusion.

Personal ownership of the story

After listeners have had opportunities to clarify their perception of the story, each one in turn shares the range of emotions they experienced during the telling. These are frequently in contrast to the teller's, who is usually only aware of one key emotion in response to the event. By highlighting the range of emotions it is possible for the teller to appreciate the number of responses that can occur, and this awareness frequently enables reconnection with various emotions that were part of the event. The teller is given the opportunity to comment on the affective responses shared by the listeners. This allows for clarification of affective reactions and comment on differences between perceptions of tellers and listeners.

This focus on feelings enables the cathartic needs of tellers and listeners to be acknowledged and addressed. In most cases this discussion and exploration is sufficient. However, sometimes tellers find this process inadequate and they remain stuck with unresolved issues. When this occurs it is worth considering the teller's past experience, which consists of previous events that continue to shape current experience. Often unresolved past experiences are impacting on the current situation. Use of spontaneous drawings, as previously outlined, can prove helpful in uncovering such issues, especially if there are unconscious elements.

Key players

The next phase in appreciating the story is to explore different perspectives of the teller's story. The group identifies who they consider to be the key players in the story. Who is important? Who played a significant role? Those named usually include people from the story itself or those introduced through discussion. It is also useful for the group to brainstorm, to move beyond these obvious choices. There may be children, parents or grandparents who are very important to the event described but who may not have been identified in the initial telling. During this phase the teller can provide further details about the story and the people involved. Through this process the teller deepens appreciation of the complexity of the experience and comes to a new awareness of the contextual elements that make up the story.

Reconstructing the story

Once key players have been identified, the group decides who are the most important people in this story. The number of people chosen must be the same as the number in the group. Each of these key players is then recorded on a small card, which is placed face down on a central table. The cards are mixed up before students each select one, and thus the role they will play. The facilitator allows a couple of minutes to enable students to move into role and then retell the story from their key player's perspective. The use of creative thinking provides a plausible context that shifts the story from single to multiple perspectives.

Debriefing and wondering

The final part of the activity is to encourage students to debrief from their roles and explore insights they have gained. In particular, listeners resume their role as peers and wonder about how they might act in a similar situation, given their new insights. It is important that this is done with sensitivity and care. This is not a time to say, 'If I were you, I would . . .'. Rather, it is a time to wonder about 'How might I act if I were in this situation?'. It is important that the group accepts responsibility for the safety and comfort of each other. The idea is to provide a range of possible alternative approaches that could be attempted in this type of situation. It is also appropriate for students to acknowledge aspects of the story where good practice or insight was evident.

At the end of this process the storyteller has the right of reply. The teller may want to comment on something that has been discussed, on feelings identified or the role-reversals that were shared. In particular, this provides opportunities to engage in conversation and explore those alternative approaches to practice that appeal. This concluding phase enables the storyteller to regain control of their story. Sometimes the teller uses this time to comment on the 'wondering' of listeners, at other times the ways in which different interpretations of the story emerged are discussed.

The following story, which was recounted by a postgraduate student working in a reflective group session, demonstrates how using this process helped her gain insight into a practice event.

> I was working as a student in an out-patient department at the local hospital and the registered nurse asked me to go and collect the next patient, an elderly lady, from the waiting room as the surgical registrar was ready to see her. After the initial greeting, I asked this lady what

she was expecting to happen at the appointment. She replied that the doctor was going to give her some ointment to make the lump on her upper lip go away. I was thinking that it was a bit strange because she was going to see a surgeon. Anyway, the doctor had a good look at the lump and said: 'It needs to be cut out and I can do it now'. The lady seemed quite vague to me and said 'Oh, OK'. The next thing the doctor asked the nurse to get a tray so they could go ahead. I felt it was all too quick – I mean I knew what this woman had been thinking. So I said to the doctor that I wondered about informed consent. He said that the patient had said it was OK to go ahead. I still felt unsure so I talked to the registered nurse – but she thought it was all right as well. I became really uneasy so I spoke to both the charge nurse and the supervisor but they both sided with the doctor and registered nurse. I still feel that she didn't know what was happening – I mean it was likely that there would be quite a big scar from the surgery – yet I was powerless to do anything, nobody would listen. I still feel really angry that no one would listen.

At the end of the story, listeners clarified the age of the patient – she was about 70 – and the teller confirmed their impression that she was alert and able to understand what was happening. The listeners then identified three key feelings that were engendered by the story: anger, frustration and powerlessness.

The group of eight students identified the key players as the patient, her husband, the student, the registrar seeing the patient, the registered nurse assisting him, the charge nurse, the supervisor and the consultant to whom the registrar was responsible.

The role-play of the student and patient provided information that was similar to that presented in the story. The registrar was imagined to be a quiet, competent person who was left to his own devices by a grateful consultant. After a busy night on call, complex surgical procedures and some uncertainty about positive outcomes, he was relieved to see a patient for whom there was a straightforward and most likely successful treatment. The student's concern about informed consent was met with a feeling of 'here we go again'. Couldn't the student appreciate that this lump could be dealt with here and now, and that the patient had agreed?

The registered nurse who assisted the registrar was presented as someone who was burnt-out because of the never-ending line of new faces that greeted her each day. She did not get on very well with the doctor but he was efficient and clear about his decisions – she certainly was not going to question him.

The charge nurse and supervisor were presented as people who were drowning in management issues and paper work. They had enough on their plates without having to worry whether a patient, who had agreed to have minor surgery, had given informed consent.

The consultant was presented as someone who was running a large department and grateful to have a competent registrar who would take responsibility for the clinic.

The patient's husband was imagined as someone who had an expectation that his wife would come home with some cream for the lump on her lip. He was anxious that she should have to go to hospital, but sure that it would turn out to be nothing serious and would not require surgery.

Once these multiple perspectives had been presented, the 'key players' identified the feelings they had experienced as part of their 'roles'. These mirrored the content of the various presentations.

Listeners then disengaged from their roles and resumed the role of peers. They 'wondered' how they would deal with a similar situation. There were a variety of suggestions that included attempting to involve the charge nurse or supervisor more directly and asking more specific questions on behalf of the patient. This suggestion was expanded upon with one of the listeners suggesting that perhaps the student could enter into an open dialogue with the patient in front of the doctor and/or the nurse. During the conversation the patient's knowledge and understanding of what was happening could be explored. It would then be possible to confirm correct assumptions and deal with misinformation or lack of information as it was revealed. A couple of listeners commented on the insights they had gained about the impact of burn-out, while another realised the importance of good working relationships with other health professionals.

The teller then had the right of reply, during which she engaged the group in a discussion related to possible implementation of the 'open dialogue' option. She felt that she had good communication skills and could manage it well. Such a comment provides a good example of the interplay between reflective practice and self-assessment.

In a session three weeks later, this student reported that she had been involved in a similar situation where she had successfully used this new technique. It had worked very well and she was able to clarify the patient's knowledge deficits and how well the patient understood the options.

Like the individual storytelling process outlined in the previous chapter, this formal group process provides students with opportunities to demonstrate how the Reflective Learning through Storytelling model can be used. Sharing a story and clarifying story details and feelings engages students with the 'noticing', 'making sense' and 'making meaning' stages of Moon's Map of Learning (1999). While these are important stages and allow students to appreciate a practice event, only surface learning is likely to occur.

When conversation related to a story moves to gaining insight into alternative perspectives, exploration of possible practice options and decisions regarding reflective outcomes, deep learning is more likely to occur. This shift demonstrates 'deep learning' as advocated by Entwistle (1996) and 'working with meaning' and 'transformative learning' as depicted in Moon's Map of Learning (1999).

Formalised reflective storytelling processes provide students with unique opportunities to learn from experience. Group storytelling enables tellers and listeners to appreciate the affective component of stories, comprehend the complexity revealed through multiple perspectives and acknowledge various alternative practice options. Working within a socio-cultural framework, the focus is on the interactive nature of learning and the importance of contextual influences on experience. Understanding storytelling from this perspective provides breadth and depth to reflective processing and enhances possible learning outcomes. Assessing outcomes, while taking associated ethical issues into account, is considered in the next chapter.

10 Ethical and Assessment Considerations

Stories provide opportunities to examine and learn from complex professional situations through reflective dialogue. Attempts to incorporate stories into learning and assessment processes can be complex, and a range of ethical issues must be considered. This chapter begins by discussing some frequently occurring ethical issues such as confidentiality, anonymity, ownership of stories, the problem of projection and presentation of practice dilemmas. Even though such issues can cause serious concern, many educators remain enthusiastic about using storytelling because of positive learning gains made by students.

As storytelling is such a useful tool to facilitate reflective learning, it is understandable that there is a desire to incorporate it into assessment processes as well. Before attempting to capture such learning through assessment tasks it is necessary to explore the relationship between learning and assessment. It is then possible to explore formative and summative assessment. The process of implementing such assessment requires decisions about who does the assessment and how it is to be managed. Both factors are likely to have a significant impact on learning outcomes and what is evidenced in summative assessment.

ETHICAL ISSUES RELATED TO STORYTELLING

When stories emerge from practice, they frequently contain a range of affective elements, concerns, questions and unresolved issues. Inviting students to process such events for reflective learning purposes may, on occasions, cause them personal distress. It is therefore important to provide students with appropriate forms of support, such as counselling. Students may also find that as they work with one story, others come to mind. How to manage the emergence of multiple student stories safely is another challenge for educators. Offering students opportunities to work with such stories in a range of ways is helpful.

When educators and students use formalised storytelling, issues of confidentiality and anonymity must be discussed prior to sharing any personal information. It is usual for students to meet prior to their first session to discuss which processes they will use and to establish ground rules. If students have not previously used the particular formalised approach that is being proposed it is helpful to provide them with exemplars to illustrate its various stages. Once students have this information they can make informed choices about their involvement.

Ground rules need to incorporate a range of issues usually addressed when sharing information in pairs or small groups, but there are additional concerns that are worthy of consideration when working with stories:

- the problem of projection;
- the issue of confidentiality;
- revealing of sensitive or personal material;
- ownership of the story;
- presentation of practice dilemmas.

PROJECTION

To enable students to engage safely in reflective learning through storytelling, it is important for educators to ensure that they have a clear understanding of the problems associated with projection. This unconscious process involves subjective information being placed on a person or thing: something from the listener's past experience is seen as existing in the teller or someone else in the story. In particular, projection assumes knowledge of attitudes and motives behind behaviour, and judgements are passed accordingly. An educator of a reflective group brought the following situation to a supervision session.

> I was facilitating a reflective session with a group of senior nursing students who were working in a hospital setting. One student, who I will call Anne, told a story to the group. She was on a morning duty and one of her patients was involved in a trial of a new wound-dressing technique. Everyone had in-service training so it was really clear what was to be done. In particular, there was an emphasis on sterile

technique. When it came time to do this dressing, one of the registered nurses from the ward said she was going to do it and Anne could watch. Well, it was really difficult because the nurse contaminated the area. She didn't seem to realise what she was doing and was explaining how she was doing things just as she had been told. Anne really didn't know what to do. She didn't know how to tell the registered nurse that she had contaminated the area.

During the discussion that followed, Anne's peers asked various questions to clarify the detail of what happened and how she felt. Eventually a range of possible approaches were outlined within the group and Anne felt she had options that could be used should a similar situation arise again.

Following the group session one of the 'listeners' to the story, Kim, came to me and said she was concerned about what happened in the story. Kim felt Anne was involved in unethical behaviour because the patient had not been given the opportunity to give informed consent or appreciate that the treatment was a trial. We had a long conversation but the only viable solution from Kim's perspective was for me, as educator, to address the 'problem' with Anne and change the reflective sessions to ensure that such an 'unethical' situation did not slip by again! Kim did not feel it was part of her role to raise such issues within the group when discussing the story.

Kim had shifted the key issue from that raised by the teller to one that obviously for some reason concerned her, and yet she did not feel confident to address this new issue in the group. Within the supervision session there was lengthy discussion regarding the problems of projection and the complications that arise because of its unconscious nature. There was dialogue about modelling ways of dealing with such difficulties in the future should such opportunities arise.

The educator had an opportunity to address the issue again a couple of weeks later in a subsequent reflective group session. She then talked about how the situation had developed, at her next supervision session.

Anne raised the issue of the wound dressing again, as she wanted to update the group on developments. As a result of feedback and questions from various staff members, including Anne, further training was made available. During this training Anne had an opportunity to 'wonder' about the difficulty of keeping to the prescribed procedure especially at the particular point where she had seen it go wrong. The instructor went over this process and there was general discussion about how to ensure correct technique. The instructor then provided every-one with equipment and they had an opportunity to try it out.

Anne shared with the reflective group how much better she felt about the whole situation and how much more confident and competent she felt about addressing such problems in the future. The educator asked the group if anyone had any further insight they wanted to share. Nothing was offered. The educator then modelled behaviour for Kim by saying, 'I have been wondering about this trial. If I came in and was caring for this patient, how would I find out about the protocol used? How could I find out what information the patients had been given and if they had given informed consent?'. Anne immediately filled in gaps; she talked about the written information given to the patients and families, how they used diagrams to ensure they understood what was happening and how they could withdraw from the programme at any stage.

The following day the educator had an opportunity to talk with Kim who raised the issue of the further information provided by Anne. Kim had been thinking about it a lot overnight and wondered if she had reacted in the way that she did because her grandmother was involved in a trial of medication some years earlier. During the trial her grandmother had suffered a heart attack and died. Although she was told that the death was not related to the trial, as a child she wondered if her grandmother might not have died if she had not been involved. The most interesting thing for Kim was that she had no conscious thought of her grandmother when engaged in earlier conversations with the educator about her concerns regarding Anne's behaviour. She also realised that she had no idea what type of information or consent was involved in her grandmother's case.

The primary safeguard against projection is awareness of its potential use by other members of the group. In particular, students need to be informed about the unconscious nature of projection and ways in which it can be manifest. However, victims of projection are often in a very vulnerable situation and therefore as an additional protection it is important to ensure all students engaged in formalised processes are alert to projections poss-ible use and ways to intervene on behalf of others. One effective inter-vention is for a group member to suggest that projection may be occurring. Educators have a particularly important role in ensuring the safety of group members, but in itself this is not sufficient as the projection may come from the educator.

Projection may occur at any stage of the reflective process, therefore as an underlying principle it is important to recognise that while stories comes from the teller's perspective, listeners or assessors hear a version based on their own assumptions and personal perceptions. Dialogue provides opportunities to discuss, question, explain and explore how stories have been heard.

CONFIDENTIALITY AND ANONYMITY

Establishing ground rules related to confidentiality and anonymity often appears deceptively simple. Usually group members are familiar with these expectations and acknowledge their importance. However, these concepts need exploring within storytelling for they apply to all the people who are part of the story as well as the experience that is shared.

Much of our work with reflective practice has occurred in relatively sparsely populated areas. Even when tellers take reasonable care in presenting information about particular individuals or situations, it is likely that someone in the group will recognise key elements and 'guess' who is involved or which situation is being presented. Most of the time this does not cause too many problems because the individual who recognises the situation is, or has been, involved in some professional capacity. However, the scenario presented in the next story highlights how easily the situation can become more complex.

A group of post graduate social work students, who were enrolled in a university paper, were introduced to storytelling as a useful way to debrief. One social worker shared a story about a couple she was seeing regularly. They had adopted a child but were not managing very well and needed a lot of support. She provided various examples of the difficulties they were having and through this process coincidentally revealed the gender of the child, the birth date and the place of birth.

One of the other social workers in the group realised that the discussion was about a child she had given up for adoption. She didn't say anything at the time but felt very distressed that her child had not been placed with a family who could offer the kind of care she had anticipated. As she thought about the incident she was disturbed that this information had been revealed in such a public forum and wondered if anyone else in the group had noticed her distress.

After thinking it through for a while the student talked to the lecturer about the situation. The lecturer was devastated that the student had been placed in such a situation, offered her support and arranged for

counselling options to be made available. The student did not want
the situation raised within the group, as she felt too vulnerable.

It seems amazing that in a relatively large city such a coincidence should
occur. However, key players from stories are often known to people in the
reflective group and may easily be identified through gender, locality or
other subtle indicators. The following examples all come from stories which
led to a person in the story being identified by someone in the group.

- A male nurse working in the paediatric ward . . .
- A nurse co ordinating the orthopaedic outpatient clinic . . .
- A male principal of a local primary school who has full-time classroom
  release . . .
- A female teacher working in an all boys school . . . .

Of course such information is not usually provided in such obvious ways.
One element may be revealed at the beginning of the story with other
elements being offered as part of clarification or explanation. Frequently,
seemingly insignificant comments that relate to favourite sports, music or
hobbies provide confirmation of identity.

As a general principle, therefore, it is usual to establish ground rules
that roles are identified rather than names, that minimal descriptive
information is provided, and that what happens in the group remains within
that setting. However, this also creates difficulties. Learners usually want
to share insights they have gained with peers or as part of assessment tasks;
this may be problematic in the context of learning through storytelling.

PRIMARY OWNERSHIP OF STORIES

It is useful to consider who learns from storytelling. Stories provide
environments in which experiences are shared. As an underlying principle
it is important to understand that stories belong to their tellers: the tellers
have *primary ownership*. The stories are the teller's to share and shape so
that they present the particular issues they are concerned with at the time.
What is told is only part of the tellers' wider reality, although through
their stories it is possible to glimpse past experience, perceptions of contexts
or environments and their views of other key players. What is learned
from stories is likely to be in line with tellers' issues and concerns, although
new and unexpected insights can be gained through reflective processing.
Therefore, when reading exemplars, listening to stories or engaging in
dialogue for the purpose of reflection or assessment, it is important for

those involved to have some sense of empathy with the tellers. This will include a desire to try and understand stories from the tellers' perspective and gain an appreciation of the issues tellers wish to explore. The tellers may want to address particular problems, seek reassurance about actions they have engaged in or discuss events that have left them confused and needing assistance. Reflective dialogue on a story or formative discussion about it should focus on clarification of details or on the tellers' intent, and others involved must take care not to pass judgement or assign blame. It is usual for listeners to offer comments, insights or suggestions to tellers based on their interpretations of stories. If tellers of original stories seek further information or clarification it is possible that 'listeners' could use examples from their own experience by way of illustration. During such interactions tellers need to respect listeners' stories as the issue of ownership is now more complex.

While it is generally accepted that the individual with *primary ownership* of the story can repeat it in other settings, care must be taken if revealing details of dialogue about the story. Such dialogue belongs to the group and needs to be treated with respect. However, insights into the teller's practice that are gained through the formalised process belong to the teller and must be available for sharing.

SECONDARY OWNERSHIP OF STORIES

Learning through storytelling can also occur by listening to stories told by others. Insights can be gained into both past and present experience. It is possible to discover new ways to understand past actions or find appropriate professional responses to situations. However, within the process of learning and when attempting to articulate learning, an interesting dilemma of ownership of stories can arise. The listener's insight and story becomes so intertwined with the teller's story that the listener has *secondary ownership* and may feel that it is necessary to retell the original story to enable new insights to be clarified or articulated.

An educator, supervising student teachers on placement, presented such a dilemma during a supervision session.

> During a formative feedback session Peter was asked by an educator to share an insight he had gained to his practice that was informed by some theoretical perspective. Peter began by recounting a story that had been shared by another student. This student shared how she had been chatting with parents of the children in her class as they dropped the children off in the morning or came to collect them in the evening.

Each time, she said hello and asked them how they were. They replied with a range of responses but she saw the interaction as primarily a conversation starter. It was not until one child started having truancy problems that she realised that the parents had been providing her with information about difficulties in the home and she had not picked up the cues. As discussion about the story proceeded, Peter realised that he had not been attending to the information the parents were providing either. After this initial insight he began thinking about not only what was said but the non-verbal cues as well. Peter re-examined communication theory, which was part of his course, and his findings caused him to bring about a change to the way he practised.

This type of scenario raises two questions:

- First, is it possible to maintain confidentiality and anonymity for the original teller and still present issues that provided insight for listeners? Frequently this requires the *secondary owner* of the story to engage in a reflective phase prior to the telling of the story. Such reflection enables the secondary owner to identify what essential elements need to be shared to enable insights or learning to be explained.

- Second, in what ways should listeners acknowledge the source of the story and how is this balanced with recognition of the personal inter-pretation that inevitably occurs? Achieving the balance between main-taining confidentiality and anonymity while providing due recognition of ownership remains a complex judgement. In this situation ground rules that have been collaboratively negotiated and fully discussed provide a useful basis to support professional judgements.

PRESENTATION OF PERSONAL OR SENSITIVE INFORMATION

A difficulty that frequently occurs when engaging in reflective work is the revelation of personal or sensitive information by students. This is of particular concern when such information is shared within a group setting, as it can leave students feeling exposed or insecure. To attempt to prevent such revealing comments being shared, it is helpful to provide guidelines and processes that assist in the differentiation between personal processing and public sharing (Brockbank and McGill, 1998). Encouraging a range of reflective techniques such as using a diary or journal or engaging in spontaneous drawing, which can be used prior to storytelling can assist students to clarify what information is appropriate to share.

PRESENTATION OF PRACTICE DILEMMAS

Stories shared during reflective processing inevitably include some scenarios or aspects of practice that are questionable. While it is important to remain aware that issues are being presented from one perspective and that projection may be occurring, the possibility of ethical dilemmas remains.

It is important that all members of a reflective group feel comfortable to own and acknowledge ethical dilemmas they perceive (Beaty, 1997). It may take time and practice for group members to become confident in this area but it is important that such concerns can be raised. Educators have a key role in modelling such behaviour.

There are two approaches that can be used either independently or sequentially in relation to practice dilemmas. The order of use will depend on the situation that is presented and individual preference.

- It must be acknowledged that there is an issue of concern. This needs to be owned as a personal concern and expressed within this framework. Using this technique enables a position to be stated without engaging in blame or criticism.

- It is also advantageous to seek further clarification of events. This may occur through formal storytelling processes or through the dialogue that follows. Exploring the context or background of stories can provide useful information, while working through multiple perspectives can throw light on other ways of viewing scenarios.

Once clarification has been gained it is possible for potential outcomes to be identified. These may arise spontaneously or emerge as part of reflective processing. Ideally tellers will discover ways in which to prevent similar situations happening in future. However, some issues or concerns may remain, and it is important that the group explores appropriate ways in which these can be addressed or reported. Opportunities for support and counselling also need to be considered as such situations may leave individuals feeling vulnerable and isolated.

Such dilemmas are more likely to occur when critique of practice is encouraged as part of the reflective processing (Fitzgerald, 1994). Development of a critical framework is presented as a likely outcome of reflective processing and an integral part of self and peer assessment (Brew, 1999; Taylor, 2000). However, some concern has been expressed about undergraduate or newly registered practitioners being encouraged to work at this level as they are being 'set up to do this difficult work without adequate preparation or indeed authority' (Fitzgerald, 1994: 77). It is therefore essential that those using reflective practice are provided with appropriate support, encouraged to explore outcomes that will impact directly on the way they practise, and that they are assisted to articulate changes to practice which they can implement. Such outcomes may still have far-reaching effects but are less likely to place students in positions where they directly challenge the workplace systems in which they are operating.

It is important to maintain balance between the necessity of addressing such complex ethical issues and the potential learning available through storytelling. Such issues need to be discussed amongst reflective-group members to ensure that they are aware of potential dangers and pitfalls. Dialogue involved in setting, re-examining and re-defining ground rules for groups provide opportunities for complex issues such as these to be addressed while ensuring the potential for learning is maintained.

ASSESSMENT AND LEARNING

Examining the relationship between assessment and learning is of fundamental importance. This relationship is shaped by the underlying philosophical approach inherent in practice. The traditional view of learning and assessment is individualistic and focuses on what individuals have learnt and what they can achieve independently.

However, educators are increasing showing interest in socio-cultural perspectives of learning (Vygotsky, 1978). Within this framework, learning does not occur in isolation, it focuses on what can be achieved with support or scaffolding. To ensure such support is appropriate it is necessary to assess what the student can achieve with minimal support and what can be achieved with maximum support. The role of the support person is to hold the complexity of the task constant and allow the student to become gradually more actively involved as competence and confidence increase. There is less interest in learning that has been internalised and is able to be used as required, unless the current learning in some way brings that knowledge into question or offers scope for the new connections to be made. If this happens, what is known once again becomes part of active learning. This constructivist approach highlights the importance of dialogue as part of learning and demands recognition of the impact of contexts on learning outcomes. Learning from experience through storytelling fits comfortably within this constructivist framework.

In contrast, the assessment practices within many higher education programmes such as degree courses continue to operate within a more individualistic approach. End-point summative assessment, in particular, focuses on what students can achieve unaided. This is more consistent with the philosophy that assumes that learning or assessment activities are carried out in isolation. This type of assessment is used to fulfil the demand to know what students can achieve unaided and assumes this will be constant in any given environment: that the quantity and quality of support available will not influence attainment. With such discrepancy between learning and assessment approaches, the validity of such assessment must be called into question, even if the detail of the aims or objectives can be seen to match the assessment tasks.

There have been attempts to bring learning and assessment processes into line. However, this is not simple and providing opportunities for dialogue is essential. Such dialogue can be demonstrated through use of formative as well as summative assessment.

FORMATIVE AND SUMMATIVE ASSESSMENT FEEDBACK

Formative assessment primarily provides opportunities to shape and develop learning (Crooks, 1988, 1993). Such feedback is likely to provide maximum impact, as students are eager to ensure their work meets the requirements of assigned tasks and is presented in acceptable ways. Because it is not high-stakes assessment it provides opportunities to try out new approaches to topics under discussion and examine different ways to address issues without worrying about errors, omissions or oversights.

To enable such feedback to be given it is necessary for both educators and students to have access to criteria and be aware of the relative importance or weighting of various aspects of assignments. Providing students with one without the other leaves them in a disadvantaged situation. It is most beneficial if students and educators establish together, when assignments are provided, what criteria will be used, and as far as possible it is important that students take the lead in this process. While educators have opportunities to comment on or add to criteria, this can be done in ways that allow students to explore the impact these additions or alterations have on their work.

Formative feedback should focus on criteria that have been agreed upon. It needs to indicate both what has been successfully achieved and what needs further development. Where criteria have been met in a minimal way, it can be helpful to identify possible improvements. It is also appropriate to comment on issues such as grammar, punctuation, tightness of argument and general editing aspects. While some educators may be concerned that such formative feedback might require them to re-write students' assignments, it is more appropriate to provide comment and a brief example. An educator recounted the following experience during supervision.

> A postgraduate-level student was seeking assistance with an assignment that had a restriction of 3,000 words. She had 6,000 words and could not work out which sections to leave out, as they were all necessary to meet the criteria that had been established for the assignment. It was noted in the feedback that her assessment was correct: the assignment did require all the aspects she had included. However, the writing style could be tightened up. Three paragraphs, chosen randomly throughout the assignment, were reworked for the student. In each case the word count was decreased significantly – from 250 to 50 words; 300 to 100; 400 to 200. When the work was returned to the student she recognised what needed to be done, worked on the remainder of the assignment and developed her editing skills.

Many educators spend considerably more time and effort in justifying their summative judgement on a piece of student work, which is likely to have significantly less impact on student behaviour, than on formative feedback. Students report feelings of anger, frustration and disappointment when educators who have been asked to provide formative feedback have not commented on content, grammar or punctuation in ways that enable change and development of an assignment. Yet educators have obviously spent considerable time working through a whole assignment during the summative assessment, noting such items as grammar issues that needed attention. If assignments are to be assessed in such detail it would seem more appropriate and effective, in terms of enabling students to change their behaviour, to provide this detailed feedback in formative ways. A briefer comment, sufficient to justify the grade awarded, could then be given as part of summative assessment.

Providing formative feedback on learning from storytelling, shared through exemplars, enables comments to be made on insights that have been articulated from experience. Of particular importance at the formative stage is feedback on the appropriateness of an exemplar that has been chosen in relation to the task students are attempting to achieve. Comment should focus on clarity of presentation, and inclusion of sufficient and appropriate detail with enough context to enable readers to grasp the point being made without providing unnecessary material or information, especially anything of a sensitive nature. Through constructive formative feedback students are provided with a safety net that can encourage articulation of learning that has occurred from reflective practice. Students may be unsure about how much to reveal, especially in relation to problems or mistakes. With particularly sensitive information it is helpful to talk with students as well as provide written comment, to ensure they are clear about how to proceed. If dialogue is possible as part of formative feedback it is also helpful to provide opportunities for students to explore other ways in which theory can be related to, or developed from, experience.

Summative assessment should also follow criteria that have been established for the grading of assignments. Having reshaped their work in response to formative feedback, students have opportunities to provide their best work for grading. While it is common for elements of norm-referenced assessment to creep into criteria-referenced processes as markers compare work to ensure reliability, care should be taken to ensure that it is the criteria that dominate when decisions are made about grades.

Criteria developed to assess exemplars that draw on storytelling experiences need to relate to specific assignments. Educators can establish criteria which provide students with opportunities to:

- demonstrate learning that has occurred,
- identify the relevance of theory that has been discussed by offering comment or critique,
- establish theory from practice.

While such assignments can take a number of forms, when working with insights gained from reflective practice it is important to include evidence of what has been achieved and/or how it was achieved. To demonstrate that insights have been gained, it is essential that such evidence is accompanied by details not only of the choices that were made but also the reasons for these choices, the theory that underpins the thinking and the new knowledge that has developed (Beaty, 1997). Of key importance is the fact that demonstration of such learning will be contextualised.

Mature students often seek opportunities for contextualisation as this enables new learning to be placed in relation to prior knowledge and past experience. Placing learning in context can have positive gains for all students as it enables the theory–practice gap to be reduced. However, from an assessment perspective, there can be some disadvantages, especially when educators insist on examining students in decontextualised ways. Such examinations are particularly difficult for students when used as summative assessments as they require that the subject matter be placed outside the practice reality.

Summative assessments can also be complicated if they include impressions and judgements that are made over a period of time when educators are working with students (Eraut, 2000). Such observations can include the ability students have to approach problems, work as members of a team, apply theory to practice or learn from the experiences of others. While students appreciate receiving positive feedback, it can be disconcerting if problems or concerns appear to be included inappropriately. A third-year nursing student shared the following story.

> I had just started working in the psychiatric area, it was my first day. I had been placed in a secure unit and I was really nervous. We had been given this big key and I seemed to spend all day locking and unlocking doors. At lunchtime I went with the registered nurse who was giving out medications. She asked me to go to the treatment room and get some pain relief tablets for one of the patients. I went and got them and we checked out the tablets for the patient. We were there chatting for quite a while and gradually the patients finished their lunch and left the dining room to go to their rooms or whatever. It must have been about 20 minutes later that I went out of the dining room and I discovered that I had left the door between the main corridor and the treatment room unlocked. The treatment room itself was locked but it was the door in-between. I must have forgotten to lock it when I got the tablets. I felt really sick. I went to the registered nurse and explained what had happened. He was great. He explained what I needed to do and came with me to check the area that had been left unlocked and then together we checked on every person in the unit – where they were and that they were OK. We chatted as we went around and he seemed to understand how strange this kind of ward was to me. I was so upset but at least I found out what to do if a door was left unlocked.

> A couple of hours later an educator arrived and asked how I was getting on. I was still feeling a bit shaken by my mistake and I was telling him about it. I explained how good the staff nurse had been showing me how to check the area and check all the patients. He seemed quite happy that I now knew what to do and didn't make any further comment until I got my summative assessment from the area about four weeks later. The educator failed me on safety because I had left a door unlocked in a secure unit. I mean it was on my first day – I never left anything unlocked again. And I knew what to do if it did happen. I would never tell an educator anything like that again. They can't be trusted!

The impact of the educator using this information in this way was significant. For the student it meant completing a further two-week placement over her holiday period or else repeating a whole semester. However, she shared her feelings with her peers who also learned to be very careful about the type of information they shared with educators. This type of story can have a major impact on students' willingness to participate in reflective practice, and therefore educators have to be very clear about their boundaries. If such information is to be used for summative assessment it is crucial to dialogue with students to ensure mutual understanding. This event also provides an example of a story having an impact beyond those who were originally involved, because other students subsequently became reluctant to share their experience.

ASSESSMENT OPPORTUNITIES

When educators use formative or summative assessment it is possible to incorporate a range of approaches that can add richness to the learning experience (Crooks, 1993) and enhance the quality of data collected to demonstrate that learning has occurred. Three main processes are required as part of assessment: setting criteria, selecting evidence and making judgements. While traditionally all three have been undertaken by educators, evidence now shows that sharing these processes with students has a positive impact on learning outcomes (Biggs, 1999). All three processes can be implemented through a range of approaches, including self-assessment, peer-assessment and assessment by educators.

Self-assessment, when used in conjunction with reflective practice, encourages students to move beyond assessment of particular skills to engage in more holistic views of practice. Through formalised storytelling students gain insight into their practice and find ways to evaluate the outcomes they achieve. Such critical thinking enables students to explore possible alternatives, plan changes that could be made and then evaluate the appropriateness of outcomes (Boud, 1995). Without reflection and self-assessment, many outcomes that are successfully achieved are not acknowledged because the focus remains on areas of difficulty or the unexpected problems that arise in practice settings.

Clarifying criteria that will be used for summative purposes can enhance self-assessment as it enables students to sharpen their appreciation of curriculum demands. From this basis it is more likely that students using self-assessment will consider appropriate evidence. If students are also offered opportunities to decide on the quality of such choices by examining the extent to which criteria have been met, appreciation of the expected learning outcomes increases substantially and enables effort to be directed toward attaining particular goals. While some educators express uncertainty about students' competence to fulfil this task, if it is supported by formative feedback and collaborative discussion with peers, there are opportunities to ensure appropriate standards are achieved.

Self-assessment is enhanced by the use of reflective dialogue because it provides opportunities to explore details of what happened and also examine what could have been different. Such evaluative judgements help students make choices about preferred ways to practise and critique options that they previously selected (Boud, 1995; Brown, 1999a).

Reflective dialogue also provides opportunities for students to engage in peer review: the feedback listeners offer to tellers during storytelling sessions is a form of formative peer-assessment. It is formative because it assists tellers to gain insight into processes that were part of their practices, as revealed through their stories, and the outcomes that tellers felt were or were not achieved. Peer-assessment provides considerable learning gains as it encourages thinking and increases confidence (Brew, 1999; Falchikov, 1986). The most helpful peer feedback enables tellers to make links between the processes that were chosen and the resulting outcomes in a given situation. Providing such feedback to peers demands that critique of practice occurs in constructive ways. Such processes not only provide useful information to tellers but also opportunities for listeners to learn about their own practice and develop 'comparative evaluative facilities for themselves' (Brown, 1999b: 8).

One role of educators facilitating reflective learning through storytelling is to encourage tellers and listeners to gain insight into their practice through self and peer-assessment. Educator's modeling of effective ways to explore and examine details of practice events is particularly important and needs to occur in an open and non-threatening environment in which alternative practice options can be explored. It is particularly helpful if examples of questioning techniques that enable clarification of specific details, motivations or consequences are also provided to students.

Another assessment role for educators is to ensure that tellers receive adequate formative feedback to develop insight into their practice. An essential aspect of such feedback is the establishment of clear boundaries around the different types of material that are appropriate for formative rather than summative assessment. Through formative feedback it is possible for educators to enable tellers to develop a deeper appreciation of their practice and assist in the construction of exemplars that provide evidence relating to criteria established for assessment tasks. This ensures that such evidence is supported by appropriate contextual and explanatory material. In addition, formative feedback can verify that evidence provided adequately articulates the reflective learning that has occurred and can be recognised through the assessment. This process is complex and usually requires that educators and students engage in dialogue to clarify the reflective processing that has occurred and the learning outcomes that have been achieved. Use of insights from reflective practice based on story-telling for assessment purposes provides a useful 'backwash' effect (Biggs, 1999) as it reinforces reflective processing and enhances learning opportunities. From the basis of formative feedback, educators can move into the role of summative assessor, being confident that both they and their students have a clear understanding of the nature of the assessment, the information that will be judged and the criteria that will be used.

The range of ethical and assessment issues addressed in this chapter is not intended to cover each and every situation that may arise. The issues have been chosen because they reflect the more frequently occurring situations that arise when engaging with students in storytelling.

When dealing with any of these situations it is important to have negotiated ground rules that inform the reflective process, provide opportunities for dialogue about stories and reflective outcomes, and establish clear boundaries that enable students and educators to remain safe while engaging in learning from experience.

11 Reflections

Support for using narrative as a learning tool to develop practice comes from diverse areas such as education, psychology, philosophy, anthropology, history, medicine and, more recently, biology. Scholars, writers, educators and practitioners from different backgrounds, and with diverse agendas, are using stories for educative purposes. By writing this book and sharing our storytelling experiences, we have attempted to contribute to the body of knowledge currently amassing around narrative forms. In this, our concluding chapter, we comment briefly on recent cautionary tales relating to reflection, describe our experience of writing this book and summarise our ideas and insights from preceding chapters.

LISTENING TO CAUTIONARY TALES

As advocates of a reflective orientation to professional preparation, we contend that formalised storytelling is a tool which enables students to reflect on their emerging practice and also enhance their capacity to manage the intricacies, uncertainties and tensions they will encounter in later professional roles (Loughran, 1996). However, we do take note of cautionary tales about the constraints and impediments to reflection. Like Larrivee (2000: 304), we acknowledge that 'the route to becoming a reflective practitioner is plagued by incremental fluctuations of irregular progress'. We also recognise that some students may find reflective processes difficult to embrace. In particular, we have noted Boud and Walker's (1998: 196) concerns regarding the lack of recognition some educators give to context when reflection is promoted in professional courses. Boud and Walker (1998) refer to context as 'the total cultural, social and political environment in which reflection takes place'. They suggest that some educators may need to consider the following factors when planning reflective activities:

- Their awareness of what elements of the cultural, institutional or disciplinary context may need to be filtered or confronted in this local context, or may be used to advantage in the learning event (i.e. a particular session in a course).

- How they can cope with the demands of the institution within which they operate.

- Their own power and the ways in which this might impact on learners singularly and collectively (p. 203).

We agree that some educators are unaware of the influence context has on learning and teaching and we have endeavoured to advance this matter in a small way, first by positioning storytelling within a constructivist framework and linking it to Vygotsky's (1978) socio-cultural theory, and second, by stressing the importance of incorporating contextual features into storytelling so they can also be explored as part of the reflective process. The approach we promote encourages students to work with their culturally situated sense-making processes, to integrate past and present learning and to attend to affective components. Our individual and group-story-telling processes, which enable students to use reflection and experience to make meaning of professional practice, are underpinned by the con-structivist principles of context, construction, collaboration and conversa-tion. However, while these processes and principles support our approach to learning, we do heed the research findings of others.

Reluctant reflectors

We were interested in Sumsion's (2000) account of reluctant reflectors who were exposed to four different forms of reflection: journal writing, revisiting practicum experiences, identification of critical incidents and discussions with critical friends. Two influences highlighted in this research were lack of student commitment to their profession, which in this study was teaching, and lack of commitment to reflection. As educators we hope that students make a commitment to their chosen programme of study when they enroll; however, as this study revealed, we cannot make this fundamental assumption. Perhaps such findings support student exposure to, and reflection on, the realities of particular professions prior to enrolment.

Variable student commitment to reflective activities raises the issue of how, when and under what conditions, and for what purpose, students are introduced to the concept of reflection and its related activities. As outlined in this text, we take a five-stage reflective storytelling approach that we think helps to overcome student attitudinal problems by presenting the concept in small, manageable and easily digestible parts. We also recognise that reflection is a concept that makes some students feel uncomfortable, but contend that their resistance to it is reduced when they are encouraged to appreciate its role in learning how to become professional.

While we have both used a variety of reflective activities in our teaching practice, including individual and collaborative journalling, we have not had the same success with these tools as with storytelling. This may be because storytelling is a familiar communication tool with aspects that do not need explanation, and can be used in many different ways, or because we have become more skilled in how we work with this particular tool. Probably it is a bit of both. This is not to say we have encountered no reluctant storytellers, but they are, to date in our experience, rare. The difficulty we most frequently come across is trying to accommodate more student stories than we have time to process appropriately.

Assessing reflective activities

A significant factor, cited by the students who were described as reluctant reflectors in Sumison's (2000) study, was the lack of assessment attached to their reflective activities, a fine example of what Crooks (1993) refers to as 'assessment driving learning'. We have addressed this issue in relation to storytelling by providing exemplars, which allow this reflective tool to be assessed without compromising students, the tool itself or its potential to achieve reflective learning outcomes.

Variable appeal

As we have already acknowledged, learning through storytelling will not appeal to every student or educator, nor will every form of storytelling evoke a constructive outcome. Because of our different backgrounds, worldviews and professional experiences, at various times, as we worked on this book, one of us would promote written storytelling over oral storytelling and vice versa. Indeed, it was only after we shifted from thinking about writing a book about telling stories, to telling stories about telling stories, that we converged in ways which enabled us to move our thinking, and therefore the book, forward.

They may also be tensions between what educators think students should learn about storytelling and how, and what students think they should be taught about it and why. To reduce these tensions, we promote storytelling in both written and oral forms. Storytelling is, after all, what human beings do naturally. It remains the most engaging and commonly used mode of interaction across and within cultures, so it makes sense to us, as educators, to use it as a reflective learning tool. We would like to see it used more frequently in formal education settings, for it is only when we connect with each other in meaningful ways, about topics that matter, that learning is truly rewarding.

When storytellers and listeners gather to work with stories in formal settings, what each student learns may differ, and this aspect worries some educators. One response would be to ask if this is not what happens regardless of the learning tool used. Another way of exploring this concern is to describe what happened to us as we worked collaboratively on this book.

DIFFERENT JOURNEYS AND POINT OF CONVERGENCE

When we began writing we thought we knew quite a lot about reflection and storytelling and that articulating it in ways that would appeal to educators and students would be a challenging but exhilarating experience. In many ways it was, not least because this is our first book. It was also the hardest work we have ever done because during our discussions and while working on drafts, we had to justify to each other why we thought in certain ways, taught from particular perspectives and believed steadfastly in certain principles. We often did this by telling each other stories and, in the process, came to the same conclusion that formalised storytelling could achieve reflective learning outcomes. However, we came to this conclusion via different paths. We initially became aware of our different journeys when we read each other's stories, which are included in Chapter 1. This difference was a reminder to us that, as individuals, we sometimes need to take different routes to get to the same place.

The students we work alongside will also have stories to share that take them on diverse journeys of learning. Some of these stories will have commonly experienced themes. Others will sit alone, but be equally valid for they will reflect a particular student's experience, from a particular point of view, at a particular time in history. Difference can be liberating when we take the time to listen to and view an aspect of the world from another person's perspective then try to understand what shaped their thinking, feelings and actions, as demonstrated in the processes we outlined in Chapters 8 and 9.

Storytelling enables us to connect with each other and, on occasions, to stand alone. In many ways storytelling, as a mode of communication and a mode of inquiry, mirrors our human need to learn from others and, on occasions, to turn inwards and learn from self. If we view the construction of knowledge as a process that involves individual and collaborative learning, we are better able to increase our potential to understand the complexities inherent in our professions, ourselves, and our relationships. Learning how to explore practice critically through reflective storytelling is a formidable task for educators and students alike, but one which we have found rewarding in every sense.

EMBRACING STORYTELLING

A good starting place for educators new to using storytelling as a learning tool is to try some of the activities we have described in Chapter 5 or to share their own practice-related stories with colleagues, using the individualised process as outlined in Chapter 8. Only when we recognise the role of narrative in the development of our own practice and in our daily lives, can we fully embrace storytelling as a student learning tool. The more we work with stories, the more likely we are to become conscious of this tool's learning potential. Sometimes this potential is transparent from the outset but more frequently it is located within the stratified pockets of our personal and professional lives.

Indeed, we have become more enthusiastic about learning through storytelling as a result of writing this book. While we had previously published aspects of our Pathways Model, our Model for Reflective Learning through Storytelling formed as we grappled with how to diagrammatically represent what we thought happened during various stages and types of storytelling. We wanted to depict how we thought learning occurred and to identify which characteristics we felt impacted on learning outcomes. Through conversations with each other, colleagues and students, intense times of self-reflection and self-inquiry, and reading the work of other advocates of narrative approaches to knowing, our ideas shifted in ways that enabled us to develop this model.

Our context for writing this book was therefore constructed from many sources, including the stories we told each other in our attempts to uncover what it was we knew intuitively and wanted to convey in an educationally sound framework. It seems appropriate that stories played a major role in our writing of this book, for, as with so many individuals, they have helped to shape our personal and professional lives. Some stories remain fragile, some are more stable, while others change as we continue to engage in self-reflection, interact with others and connect with the contexts which directly and indirectly influence our lives. We also influence these contexts, given the nature of symbiotic relationships.

Another context that significantly impacted on the shape of this book was the literature on learning and reflection. It was in this arena that we found Moon's (1999) Map of Learning, which we then incorporated, along with Entwistle's (1988, 1996) surface and deep learning approaches, into our Model of Reflective Learning through Storytelling. We also attempted to link ideas we referred to in this text with storytelling: socio-cultural learning (Vygotsky, 1978), making meaning from experience (Schön, 1991), reflective dialogue (Brookfield, 1995), critical thinking (Kemmis, 1985), feelings (Boud, Keogh and Walker, 1985), transformative learning (Mezirow, 1981) and cultural contexts (Bishop and Glynn, 1999). To our delight, we discovered that each aspect could be connected through the use of formalised storytelling processes, leading us to surmise that this tool has significant learning potential in higher education contexts.

STORYTELLING AS THEORY OF LEARNING

If, as Van Manen (1991) maintains, storytelling is 'a form of everyday theorising' (p. 369) and if we, as educators, can facilitate student learning by using this reflective tool, perhaps we can better prepare them to manage the transition from student to practitioner. Mattingly (1991: 236) puts it this way:

> Storytelling and story analysis can facilitate a kind of reflecting that is often difficult to do, a consideration of those ordinarily tacit constructs that guide practice. Stories point towards deep beliefs and assumptions that people often cannot tell in propositional ways or denotive form, the 'personal theories' and deeply held images that guide their actions.

Viewing storytelling in this way provides ample opportunities for educators to alert students to alternative assumptions, models and theories. Using processes such as meta-analysis, which is outlined in Chapter 7, we can challenge ourselves, and the students we work with, to approach stories from many positions and perspectives. By doing so, we are all likely to become more effective critical users of story, and more confident that our interpretations and meaning-making will be as responsible as we can make them.

It is our contention that when we encourage students to articulate and process experience through storytelling we provide them with opportunities to clarify and question their assumptions, one of the hallmarks of a reflective practitioner. If educators and students work and learn together in this way, we think, like Brookfield (1995), the result is learning experiences that are more challenging, interesting and stimulating to students. Moreover formalised storytelling, with its emotional resonance and capacity to reveal the expected alongside the unexpected, enables both educators and students to deepen their understanding of self in the process of developing practice. As Webb (1996: 101) succinctly notes in his treatise on authentic educator/student relationships:

> When seeking an authentic staff development or teacher–learner relationship there is also the expectation that both parties will be changed. When we interact with each we do so at more than an instrumental level: we communicate with others at a (total) emotional level. We do so in order not simply to develop or teach others, but also in search for ourselves. We extend our understanding and humanity in our development and teaching relationships.

When we began writing this book we believed that storytelling was a powerful learning tool and had a significant role to play in higher education contexts. We draw our story to a close by emphasising that, from our perspective, when we tell our own practice stories and listen to those of others, then work together to process them deeply and critically, we connect in ways which enrich self, relationship and practice. Through these connections we construct new knowledge and advance our understanding of the relationships we construct and are constructed by. For these reasons we end our journey convinced that storytelling can, and should, be viewed as a theory of learning.

References

Adams, H. (1994). Teaching as assisted performance in the zone of proximal development: Implications for teacher education. Paper presented at the State of the Art in Higher Education Conference, Cape Town, South Africa.

Adams, P., Clark, J., Codd, J., O'Neill, A., Openshaw, R. & Waitere-Ang, H. (2000). *Education and society in Aotearoa New Zealand.* Palmerston North: Dunmore Press.

Alterio, M. G. (1998). Telling our professional stories. Unpublished MA Thesis, University of Otago, Dunedin, New Zealand.

Alterio, M. G. (1999a). Tell your side of the story. *The Times Higher Education Supplement*, No. 1, 380.

Alterio, M. G. (1999b). Using formalised storytelling as a professional development tool. Paper presented at the National Staff Educational Development Association and the Society for Research in Higher Education Conference, Research and Practice in Educational Development(s): Exploring the Links, Grantham, United Kingdom.

Argyris, C. & Schön, D. (1974). *Theory in practice: Increasing professional effectiveness.* San Francisco: Jossey Bass, Inc.

Arlidge, J. (2000). Constructivism: Is anyone making meaning in New Zealand adult and vocational education? *New Zealand Journal of Adult Learning,* 28(1), 32–49.

Atkins, S. & Murphy, K. (1993). Reflection: A review of the literature. *Journal of Advanced Nursing,* 18, 1188–1192.

Atkinson, T. & Claxton, G. (2000). *The intuitive practitioner: On the value of not always knowing what one is doing.* Buckingham: Open University Press.

Barthes, R. (1977). Introduction to the structural analysis of narratives. In R. Barthes (Ed.), *Image, music, text,* (S. Heath, Trans). London: Fontana/Collins.

Beatty, B. (2000). Pursuing the paradox: Emotion and educational leadership. Paper presented to the New Zealand Educational Administration Society on the occasion of the First Inaugural NZEAS Visiting Scholar Programme, November, New Zealand.

Beaty, L. (1997). Developing your teaching practice through reflective practice. *SEDA Special* No. 5, Birmingham: Staff and Educational Development Association.

Belenky, M., Clinchy, B., Goldberger, N. & Tarule, J. (1986). *Women's ways of knowing: The development of self, voice and method.* New York: Basic Books.

Belmont, J. (1989). Cognitive strategies and strategic learning. *American Psychologist* 82(3), 402–7.

Benner, P. (1984*). From novice to expert.* Menlo Park, California: Adaison-Wesley.

Benner, P. & Tanner, C. (1987). Clinical judgement: How expert nurses use intuition. *American Journal of Nursing,* 87, 23–31.

Bernays, A. & Painter, P. (1990). *What If? Writing exercises for fiction writers.* New York: Harper Perennial.

Biggs, J. (1999). *Teaching for quality learning at university.* Buckingham: Society for Research into Higher Education & Open University Press.

Bishop, R. (1996). *Collaborative research stories: Whakawhanaungatanga.* Palmerston North: Dunmore Press.

Bishop, R. (2000). Changing power relations in education: Kaupapa Maori messages for mainstream institutions. Paper presented at the DEANZ conference Supporting the Learner through Open, Flexible and Distance Strategies: Issues for Pacific Rim Countries, 27–29 April, Dunedin, New Zealand.

Bishop, R. (2001). Changing power relations in education: Kaupapa Maori messages for mainstream institutions. In C. McGee & D. Fraser (Eds), *The professional practice of teaching* (2nd Edition). Palmerston North: Dunmore Press.

Bishop, R. & Glynn, T. (1999). *Culture counts: Changing power relations in Education.* Palmerston North: Dunmore Press.

Boud, D (1995). *Enhancing learning through self-assessment.* London: Kogan Page.

Boud, D., Cohen, R. & Walker, D. (1993). *Using experience for learning.* Buckingham: Society for Research into Higher Education & Open University Press.

Boud, D., Keogh, R. & Walker, D. (1985). *Reflection: Turning experience into learning*. London: Kogan Page.

Boud, D. & Walker, D. (1998). Promoting reflection in professional courses: The challenge of context. *Studies in Higher Education,* 23 (2), 191–206.

Boyd, E. & Fales, A. (1983). Reflective Learning: Key to learning experience. *Journal of Humanistic Psychology,* 23 (2), 99–117.

Brew, A. (1999). Towards autonomous assessment: Using self-assessment and peer-assessment. In S. Brown & A. Glasner (Eds), *Assessment matters in higher education*. Philadelphia: Society for Research into Higher Education and Open University Press.

Brockbank, A. & McGill, I. (1998). *Facilitating reflective learning in Higher Education*. Buckingham: Society for Research into Higher Education & Open University Press.

Brody, C., Witherell, C., McDonald, K. & Lundblad, R. (1991). Story and voice in the education of professionals. In C. Witherell & N. Noddings (Eds), *Stories lives tell: Narrative and dialogue in education*. New York: Teachers College Press.

Brookfield, S. D. (1995). *Becoming a critically reflective teacher*. San Francisco: Jossey-Bass, Inc.

Brookfield, S. & Preskill, S. (1999). *Discussion as a way of teaching*. Buckingham: Society for Research into Higher Education & Open University Press.

Brown, A. & Palincsar, A. (1986*). Guided cooperative learning and individual knowledge acquisition* (Technical Report 372, ED 270738), Cambridge, MA: Illinois University Centre for the Study of Reading.

Brown, A. & Reeve, R. (1985). *Bandwidths of competence: The role of supportive contexts in learning and development* (Technical Report No. 336, ED 260372), Cambridge, MA: Illinois University Centre for the Study of Reading.

Brown, S. (1999a). Assessing practice. In S. Brown & A. Glasner (Eds), *Assessment matters in higher education*. Philadelphia: Society for Research in Higher Education and Open University Press.

Brown, S. (1999b). Institutional strategies for assessment. In S. Brown & A. Glasner (Eds), *Assessment matters in higher education*. Philadelphia: Society for Research in Higher Education and Open University Press.

Brown, S. & Race, P. (1997). *Staff development in action: A compendium of staff development resources and suggestions on how to use them*. SEDA Paper 100, Birmingham: Staff and Educational Development Association.

Bruner, E. (1986). Ethnography as narrative. In E. M. Bruner & V. Turner (Eds), *The anthropology of experience.* Urbana: University of Illinois Press.

Bruner, J. (1983). *In search of mind: Essays and autobiography.* New York: Harper Row.

Bruner, J. (1985). Narrative and paradigmatic modes of thought. In E. Elliot (Ed.), *Learning and teaching the ways of knowing.* Chicago: National Society for the Study of Education.

Bruner, J. (1986). *Actual minds, possible worlds.* Cambridge, MA: Harvard University Press.

Bruner, J. (1987). Life as narrative. *Social research,* 54, 11–32.

Butler, J. (1994). From action to thought: The fulfilment of human potential. In J. Edwards (Ed.), *Thinking: Interdisciplinary perspectives.* Victoria: Hawker Bronlow Education.

Byatt, A. S. (2000). *On histories and stories, selected essays.* London: Chatto & Windus.

Casey, K. (1998). The narrative in education. In M. Applie (Ed.), *Review of research in education,* 21, 211–254, AERA, Washington DC.

Chaille, C. & Britain, L. (1991). *The young child as a scientist: A constructivist approach to early childhood science education.* New York: HarperCollins.

Churchman, C. (1971). *The design of inquiring systems.* New York: Basic Books.

Clandinin, D. (1985). Personal practical knowledge: A study of teachers' classroom images, *Curriculum Inquiry,* 15 (4), 361–385.

Clandinin, D. J. (1993). Creating new spaces for women: Restorying teacher education. In D. J. Clandinin, A. Davies., P. Hogan & B. Kennard (Eds), *Learning to teach: Teaching to learn: Stories of collaboration in teacher education.* New York: Teachers College Press.

Clandinin D. & Connelly, F. (1998). Stories to live by: Narrative understandings of school reform. *Curriculum Inquiry,* 28(2) 149–164.

Clifford, J. (1986). On ethnographic allegory. In J. Clifford & G. Marcus (Eds), *Writing culture.* Berkley: University of California Press.

Coutts-Jarman, J. (1993). Using reflection and experience in nurse education. *British Journal of Nursing,* 2 (1), 77–80.

Cowan, J. (1998). *On becoming an innovative university teacher.* Buckingham: Society for Research into Higher Education & Open University Press.

Criticos, C. (1983). Experiential learning and social transformation for a post-apartheid learning future. In D. Boud., R. Cohen & D. Walker

(Eds), *Using experience for learning*. Buckingham: Society for Research into Higher Education & Open University Press.

Crooks, T. (1988). The impact of classroom evaluation practices on students. *Review of Educational Research*, 58(4) 438–481.

Crooks, T. (1993). *Assessing student performance*. NSW, Australia: HERDSA Publication.

Dadds, M. (1993). Using reflection and experience in nurse education. *Educational Action Research*, 2(1), 287–305.

Didion, J. (1979). *The white album*. New York: Simon and Schuster.

Diekelmann, N. (1990). Nursing education: Caring, dialogue and practice. *Journal of Nursing*, September, 29(7), 300–305.

Diekelmann, N. (1992). Learning-as-testing: A Heideggerian hermeneutical analysis of the life experiences of students and teachers in nursing. *Advanced Nursing Science*, 14(3), 72–83.

Dilthey W. (1977). Ideas concerning a descriptive and analytic psychology. In W. Dilthey, *Descriptive psychology and historical understanding* (Translated by R. Zaner and K. Helges). The Hague: Martinus Nijoff. (Original work published in 1894.)

Eckhartsberg, R. (1981). Maps of the mind. In R. Vaille & R. von Eckhartsberg (Ed.), *The metaphors of consciousness*. New York: Plenum.

Entwistle, N. (1988). *Styles of learning*, Edinburgh: David Fulton.

Entwistle, N. (1996). Recent research on student learning and the learning environment. In J. Tait & P. Knight (Eds), *The management of independent learning*. London: SEDA/Kogan Page Limited.

Eraut, M. (1994). *Developing professional knowledge and competence*. London: Falmer Press.

Eraut, M. (2000). The intuitive practitioner: A critical overview. In T. Atkinson & G. Claxton (Eds), *The intuitive practitioner: On the value of not always knowing what one is doing*. Buckingham: Open University Press.

Erickson, E. (1975). *Life history and the historical moment*. New York: W. W. Norton.

Falchikov, N. (1986). Product comparisons and process benefits of collaborative peer group and self assessments. *Assessment and evaluation in higher education*, 11(1), 146–65.

Farrow, A. (2000). Creative planning in the workplace. A workshop presented at the University of Victoria, Wellington.

Fitzgerald, M (1994). Theories of reflection for learning. In A. Palmer, S. Burns & C. Bulman (Eds), *Reflective practice in nursing*. Oxford: Blackwell Science Limited.

Fosnot, C. (1996) (Ed.). *Constructivism: Theory perspectives and practice.* New York: Teachers College.

Freedman, J. & Combs, G. (1996). *Narrative therapy: The social construction of preferred realities.* New York: Norton.

Freire, P. (1970). *Cultural action for freedom.* Harmondsworth: Penguin Books.

Fried, R. (1995). *The passionate teacher.* Boston: Beacon Press.

Friend, L. (2000). Guilty or not guilty: Experiencing and understanding Sweetie's guilt as dissatisfaction. In J. Schroeder & C. Otnes (Eds), Proceedings of the Fifth Conference on Gender, Marketing and Consumer Behaviour (157–173). Urbana, IL: The University of Illinois Printing Services.

Fry, H., Ketteridge, S. & Marshall, S. (1999). *A handbook for teaching and learning in higher education.* London: Kogan Page Limited.

Fulford, R. (2000). *The triumph of narrative: Storytelling in the age of mass culture.* New York: Broadway Books.

Furth, G. (1988). *The secret world of drawing: Healing through art.* Boston: Sigo Press.

Gallimore, R. & Tharp, R. (1990). Teaching mind in society: Teaching, schooling, and literate discourse. In L. Moll (Ed.), *Vygotsky and Education.* New York: Cambridge University Press.

Gibbs, G. (1988). *Learning by doing: A guide to teaching and learning methods.* Oxford: Further Education Unit, Oxford Polytechnic.

Gilligan, C. (1982). *In a different voice: Psychological theory and women's development.* Cambridge, MA: Harvard University Press.

Goodman, J. (1984). Reflection and teacher education: A case study and theoretical analysis. *Interchange,* 15(3), 89–26.

Graham, I. (1998). Understanding the nature of nursing through reflection: A case study approach. In C. Johns & D. Freshwater (Eds), *Transforming nursing through reflective practice.* Oxford: Blackwell Science.

Grant, B. & Friend, L. (1996). Analysing leisure experiences through 'memory work'. In D. Rowe & P. Brown (Eds), *Proceedings of the 1997 Australian & New Zealand Association for Leisure Studies Conference* (65–70). Newcastle, Australia: Australian and New Zealand Association for Leisure Studies and the Department of Leisure and Tourism Studies, the University of Newcastle.

Greene, M. (1996). A constructivist perspective on teaching and learning in the arts. In C. Fosnot (Ed.), *Constructivism: Theory perspectives and practice.* New York: Teachers College.

Grumet, M. (1988). *Bitter milk: Women and teaching.* Amherst: University of Massachusetts.

Gudmundsdottir, S. (1995). The narrative nature of pedagogical content knowledge. In H. McEwan & K. Egan (Eds), *Narrative in teaching, learning, and research.* New York: Teachers College, Columbia University.

Habermas, J. (1971). *Knowledge and human interests.* Boston: Beacon Press.

Habermas, J. (1987). *Knowledge and human interests* (Translated by J. Shapiro). Cambridge: Polity Press.

Haigh, N. (2000). Teaching teachers about reflection and ways of reflecting. *Waikato Journal of Education,* 6, 87–98.

Hardy, B. (1977). Towards a poetics of fiction: An approach through narrative. In M. Meek, A. Warlow & G. Barton (Eds), *The cool web: The patterns of children's reading.* London: The Bodley Head.

Hargeaves, A. (1994). *Changing teachers changing times.* London: Cassel.

Harrison (1962) cited by Dadds, M. (1993). Using reflection and experience in nurse education. *Educational Action Research,* 2(1), 287–305.

Hart, B. (1995). Reauthoring the stories we work by: Situating the narrative approach in the presence of the family of therapists. *Australian and New Zealand Journal of Family Therapy,* 16(4), 181–189.

Hatton, N. & Smith, D. (1995). Reflection in teacher education: Towards definition and implementation. *Teaching and Teacher Education,* 11, 33–49.

Head, J. & Sutton, C. (1985). Language and commitment. In L. West & A. Pines (Eds), *Cognitive structure and conceptual change.* New York: Academic Press.

Hedegaard, M. (1990). The zone of proximal development as basis for instruction. In L. Moll (Ed.), *Vygotsky and Education.* New York: Cambridge University Press.

Heron, J. (1979) *Co-counselling.* Guildford: Human Potential Resource Group, University of Surrey.

Heron, J. (1981) Self and peer assessment. In T. Bouydell & M. Pedlar (Ed.), *Handbook of management self-development.* London: Gower.

Heron, J. (1989). *The facilitator's handbook.* London: Kogan Page Limited.

Holly, M. L. (1984). *Keeping a personal/professional journal.* Victoria: Deakin University Press.

Jackson, P. (1995). On the place of narrative in teaching. In H. McEwan & K. Egan (Eds), *Narrative in teaching, learning, and research.* New York: Teachers College, Columbia University.

Johns, C. (1998). Opening the doors of perception. In C. Johns & D. Freshwater (Eds), *Transforming nursing through reflective practice.* Oxford: Blackwell Science.

Johns, C. & Hardy, H. (1998). Voice as a metaphor for transformation through reflection, In C. Johns & D. Freshwater (Eds), *Transforming nursing through reflective practice.* Oxford: Blackwell Science.

Jonassen, D., Davidson, M., Collins, M., Campbell, J. & Haag, B. B. (1995). Constructivism and computer-mediated communication. *American Journal of Distance Education,* 9(2) 7–26.

Josselson, R. (1995). Imagining the real: Empathy, narrative, and the dialogic self. In R. Josselson & A. Lieblich (Eds), *Interpreting experience: The narrative study of lives.* California: Sage Publications Inc.

Josselson, R. & Lieblich, A. (1995). *Interpreting experience: The narrative study of lives.* California: Sage Publications Inc.

Jung, C. (1926). *Psychological types.* New York: Kegan Paul, Trench, Trubner & Co Limited.

Jung, C. (1963). *Modern man in search of a soul.* New York: Harcourt Brace & World.

Kalantzis, M. & Cape, B. (1999). Multicultural education: Transforming the mainstream. In S. May (Ed.), *Critical multiculturalism: Rethinking multicultural and antiracism education.* London: Falmer Press.

Keller, C. (1986). *From a broken web: Separation, sexism and self.* Boston: Beacon Press.

Kemmis, S. (1985). Action research and the politics of reflection. In D. Boud, R. Keogh & D. Walker (Eds), *Reflection: Turning experience into learning.* London: Kogan Page.

Kolb, D. (1984). *Experiential learning: Experience as the source of learning and development.* New Jersey: Prentice Hall.

Laing, M. (1993). Gossip: Does it play a role in the socialization of nurses? *IMAGE: Journal of Nursing Scholarship,* 25(1), 37–43.

Larrivee, B. (2000). Transforming teaching practice: becoming the critically reflective teacher. *Reflective Practice,* 1(3), 293–307.

Lauritzen, C. & Jaeger, M. (1997). *Integrating learning through story: The narrative curriculum.* New York: Delmar Publishers.

Lodge, D. (1990). Narration with words. In H. Barlow, C. Blakemore & M. Weston-Smith (Eds), *Images and understanding.* Cambridge, UK: Cambridge University Press.

Lopez, B. (1987). *Arctic dreams.* New York: Bantam Books.

Loughran, J. (1996). *Developing reflective practice: Learning about teaching and learning through modelling.* London: Falmer Press.

Lumby, J. (1998). Transforming nursing through reflective practice. In C. Johns & D. Freshwater (Eds), *Transforming nursing through reflective practice*. Oxford: Blackwell Science.

McCormack, C. & Pamphilon, B. (1998). The balancing act. A paper presented at the conference Winds of Change: An international conference on women and the culture of universities, Sydney 13–17 July.

McDrury, J. (1996). Self assessment and reflective practice. Unpublished PhD thesis. University of Otago, Dunedin.

McDrury, J. & Alterio, M.G. (2001). Achieving reflective learning using storytelling pathways. *Innovations in Education and Training International,* 38(1), 63–73.

McEwan, H. (1995). Narrative understanding in the study of teaching. In H. McEwan & K. Egan, *Narrative in teaching, learning, and research.* New York: Teachers College, Columbia University.

McEwan, H. & Egan, K. (1995). *Narrative in teaching, learning, and research.* New York: Teachers College, Columbia University.

McGee, C. & Fraser, D. (Eds) (2001) *The professional practice of teaching* (2nd Edition). Palmerston North: Dunmore Press.

MacIntyre, A. (1981). *After virtue.* Notre Dame, IN: University of Notre Dame Press.

Manning, B. & Payne, B. (1993). A Vygotskian-based theory of teacher cognition: Toward the acquisition of mental reflection and self-regulation. *Teaching and Teacher Education*, 9(4), 361–371.

Mattingly, C. (1991). Narrative reflections on practical actions: Two learning experiments in reflective storytelling. In D. Schön (Ed.), *The reflective turn: Case studies in and on educational practice.* New York: Teachers College Press.

Mezirow, J. (1981). A critical theory of adult learning and education. *Adult Education,* 32(1), 3–24.

Mezirow, J. (1990). *Fostering critical reflection in adulthood.* San Francisco: Jossey-Bass.

Mink, L. (1978). Narrative form as a cognitive instrument. In R. Canary & H. Kozicki (Eds), *The writing of history.* Madison: University of Wisconsin Press.

Moll, L. (1990) (Ed.). *Vygotsky and education.* New York: Cambridge University Press.

Monk, G., Winslade, J., Crocket, K. & Epston, D. (Eds) (1997). *Narrative therapy in practice: The archaeology of hope.* San Francisco: Jossey-Bass Inc.

Moon, J. (1999). *Reflection in learning and professional development.* London: Kogan Page Limited.

Moon, J. (2001). *Short courses and workshops: Improving the IMPACT of learning, training and professional development.* London: Kogan Page Limited.

Mulligan, J. (1993). Activating internal processes in experiential learning. In D. Boud, R. Cohen & D. Walker (Eds), *Using experience for learning.* Buckingham: Society for Research into Higher Education & Open University Press.

Nias, J. & Groundwater, S. (1988). *The enquiring teacher.* Lewes: Falmer Press.

Noddings, N. & Witherell, C. (1991). Epilogue: Themes remembered and foreseen. In C. Witherell & N. Noddings (Eds), *Stories lives tell: Narrative and dialogue in education.* New York: Teachers College Press.

Pagano, J. (1991). Moral Fictions: The dilemma of theory and practice. In C. Witherell and N. Noddings (Eds), *Stories lives tell: Narrative and dialogue in education.* New York: Teachers College Press.

Parkin, M. (1998). *Tales for trainers: Using stories and metaphor to facilitate learning.* London: Kogan Page Limited.

Pendlebury, S. (1995). Reason and story in wise practice. In H. McEwan & K. Egan (Eds), *Narrative in teaching, learning and research.* New York: New York Teachers College Press.

Philips, D (1997a). Adding nuances: Or copying the perfect country-western song. *Issues in Education,* 3(2), 273–285. www.epnet.com/ehost/login.html

Philips, D. (1997b). How, why, what, when and where: Perspectives in constructivism in psychology and education. *Issues in Education,* 3(2), 151–195. www.epnet.com/ehost/login.html

Polanyi, M. (1967). *The tacit dimension.* New York: Doubleday and Co.

Polkinghorne, D. (1988). *Narrative knowing and the human sciences.* Albany: State University of New York Press.

Postle, D. (1983). Putting the heart back into learning. In D. Boud, R. Cohen & D. Walker (Eds), *Using experience for learning.* Buckingham: Society for Research into Higher Education & Open University Press.

Race, P. (1999) *2000 Tips for Lecturers.* London: Kogan Page.

Ramsden, P. (1992). *Learning to teach in Higher Education.* London: Routledge.

Ratner, H. & Stettner, L. (1991). Thinking and feeling: Putting Humpty Dumpty together again. *Merrill-Palmer Quarterly,* 37(1), 1–26.

Reason, P. & Hawkins, P. (1988). Story telling as inquiry. In P. Reason

(Ed.), *Human inquiry in action: Developments in new paradigm research*. London: Sage Publications.

Ricoeur, P. (1984). *Time and narrative*. Chicago: University of Chicago Press.

Rosaldo, R. (1989). *Culture and truth*. Boston: Beacon Press.

Sandelwoski, M. (1991). Telling stories: Narrative approaches in qualitative research. *Nursing Scholarship*, 23(3), 161–166.

Schafer, R. (1981). *Narrative actions in psychoanalysis*. Worcester, MA: Clark University Press.

Schön, D. (1983). *The reflective practitioner: How professionals think in action*. New York: Basic Books Inc.

Schön, D. (1987). *Educating the reflective practitioner*. New York: Jossey Bass.

Schön, D. (1991). *The reflective turn: Case studies in and on educational practice*. New York: Teachers College Press.

Shor, L. & Freire, P. (1987). *A pedagogy for liberation: Dialogues on transforming education*. Westport, CT: Bergen and Garvey/Greenwood Press.

Shotter, J. (1995). Dialogue: Social constructionism and radical constructivism. In L. Steffe & J. Gale (Ed.), *Constructivism in education*. Hillsdale, NJ: Lawrence Ehrlbaum.

Smagorinsky, P. (1995). The social construction of data: Methodological problems of investigating learning in the zone of proximal development. *Review of Educational Research*, 65(3), 191–212.

Smith, A. B. (1998). *Understanding children's development* (4th Edition). Wellington: Bridget Williams.

Smith, L. (2001). The interface of therapy, culture and lifestyle: Bringing cultural narratives into the therapy room. www.adfq.org/smith.html

Smolucha, L. & Smolucha, F. (1989). A Vygotskian perspective on critical thinking. Paper presented at the Conference on Science and Technology for Education in the 1990s: Soviet and American Perspectives, Meadville.

Spence, D. (1982). *Narrative truth and historical truth: Meaning and interpretation in psychoanalysis*. New York: Norton.

Spouce, J. (1998). Scaffolding student learning in clinical practice. *Nurse Education Today*, 18(4), 259–66.

Steward, D. (1995). *Beginning writers in the zone of proximal development*. Hillsdale, New Jersey: Lawrence Erlbaun Ass. Publishers.

Stockhausen, L. (1992). Reflections in clinical education. Paper presented at Reflective Practice in Higher Education Mini Conference. 11–13 July, Grace College, University of Queensland.

Sumsion, J. (2000). Facilitating reflection: A cautionary account. *Reflective practice,* 1(2), 199–214.

Tappan, M. & Brown, L. (1991). Stories told and lessons learned: Towards a narrative approach to moral development and moral education. In C. Witherell & N. Noddings (Eds), *Stories lives tell: Narrative and dialogue in education.* New York: Teachers College Press.

Taylor, B. (1998). Locating a phenomenological perspective of reflective nursing and midwifery practice by contrasting interpretive and critical reflection. In C. Johns & D. Freshwater (Eds), *Transforming nursing through reflective practice.* Oxford: Blackwell Science.

Taylor, B. (2000). *Reflective practice: A guide for nurses and midwives.* NSW, Australia: Allen & Unwin.

Tharp, R. & Gallimore, R. (1988). *Rousing minds to life.* Cambridge: Cambridge University Press.

Tudge, J. (1990). Collaborative problem solving in the zone of proximal development. Paper presented at the Annual Symposium of the Jean Piaget Society, Philadelphia.

Tudge, J. (1991). Peer collaboration: The case for treating the dyad as the unit of analysis. Paper presented at the Biennial Meeting of the Society for Research in Child Development, Seattle, April 18–20.

Van der Veer, R. & Valsiner, J. (1994). *The Vygotsky reader.* Oxford: Blackwell.

Van Manen, M. (1977). Linking ways of knowing to ways of being. *Curriculum Inquiry,* 6, 205–208.

Van Manen, M. (1991). *The tact of teaching: The meaning of pedagogical thoughtfulness.* New York: Albany State University of New York Press.

Vygotsky, L. (1978). *Mind in society: The development of higher psychological processes.* In M. Cole, V. John-Steiner, S. Scribner. & E. Souberman (Eds), Cambridge, MA: Harvard University Press.

Vygotsky, L. (1987). Thinking and speech. In Rieber, R. W & Carton A.S (Eds) (1987). *The collected works of L.S Vygotsky,* New York: Plenum Press.

Walton, T. & Toomay, M. (2000). *The writer's path: A guidebook for your creative journey.* California: Ten Speed Press.

Webb, G. (1996). *Understanding staff development.* Buckingham: Society for Research into Higher Education and Open University Press.

Wells, B. (1986). *The meaning makers.* Portsmouth, NH: Heinemann Educational Books.

Welty, E. (1984). *One writer's beginnings.* Cambridge, MA: Harvard University Press.

White, H. (1973). *Metahistory: The historical imagination in nineteenth century Europe.* Baltimore: Johns Hopkins University Press.

White, H. (1981). *The content of the form: Narrative discourse and historical representation.* Baltimore: Johns Hopkins University Press.

White, J. (1991). War stories: Invitations to reflect on practice. In B. Tabachnick & K. Zeichner (Eds), *Issues and practices in inquiry-orientated teacher education.* London: Falmer Press.

White, M. & Epston, D. (1990). *Narrative means to therapeutic ends.* New York: Norton.

Wilber, K. (1981). *Up from Eden: A transpersonal view of human evolution.* Garden City: Doubleday/Anchor.

Wilson, B., Teslow, J. and Taylor, L. (1993). Instructional design perspectives on mathematics education with reference to Vygotsky's theory of social cognition. *Focus on Learning Problems in Mathematics,* 15(2&3) 65–86. www.cudenver.edu/~bwilson

Winter, R., Buck, A. & Sobiechowska, P. (1999). *Professional experience and the investigative imagination: The ART of reflective writing.* London: Routledge.

Witherell, C. (1991). The self in narrative: A journey into paradox. In C. Witherell & N. Noddings (Eds) (1991). *Stories lives tell: Narrative and dialogue in education.* New York: Teachers College Press.

Witherell, C. & Noddings, N. (Eds) (1991). *Stories lives tell: Narrative and dialogue in education.* New York: Teachers College Press.

Name Index

Subject Index

Biographical Notes

Janice McDrury currently works as an educator and health researcher at Otago Polytechnic, Dunedin, New Zealand. She has 17 years' experience as a nurse educator and is presently a Senior Lecturer. Her use of storytelling developed when she recognised its ability to surface multiple perspectives of practice events. Her PhD studies were in the area of Self-Assessment and Reflective Practice.

Maxine Alterio currently works as a staff development coordinator at Otago Polytechnic, Dunedin, New Zealand. In her role she encourages practitioners from a range of disciplines to use formalised storytelling processes to advance their practice. She is also a prize-winning short story writer, with work published in literary magazines, journals and edited collections both in New Zealand and the United Kingdom.

Addresses for Correspondence
Dr Janice McDrury
Senior Lecturer
Otago Polytechnic
Private Bag 1910
DUNEDIN
New Zealand
Email: JaniceM@tekotago.ac.nz

Maxine Alterio
Staff Development Coordinator
Otago Polytechnic
Private Bag 1910
DUNEDIN
New Zealand
Email: Maxaa@tekotago.ac.nz